Contents telepathically received from the Pleiadians and the Galactic Confederation

Written By Ishtar Antares of Ljubljana Slovenia 1993-2009

Published by MusiVation International June 2009
and Ishtar Antares
E mail antarion@volja.net website www.aurora2012.net



ISBN .... 978-1-890679-10-1



Printed in the United States of America
Front cover by Neno
For wholesale quantities contact MusiVation International
1(858) 268 8688
P O Box 12933 La Jolla CA USA 92039

First Edition 2009

This is a reference work based upon telepathically received contents and other sources by the author during the Earth time period of 1993 - 1995 and 2003 to 2009 with additional materials from the authors sources and files as well as updates from the original telepathic sources. Opinions expressed herein are not necessarily those of the publisher or the author.

# TABLE OF CONTENTS

# INTRODUCTION BY MICHELE BLOOD

I have been teaching, writing books and speaking globally about positive thinking, metaphysics and spirituality since 1990. I have co written books and shared the stage with many amazing souls including Bob Proctor, Dr Deepak Chopra, Dr Wayne Dyer and met real Enlightenment. So my background is such that I have a very open mind to anything mystical...and yet if someone started speaking about aliens etc I did not disbelieve but I had no interest in pursuing that type of path. In fact I would run a million miles away from 'those types' if I could. I am saying this because if like me you have had no interest before in anything that 'out there' then please keep an open mind this time and read this book. NOW is the time to be open!

The reason I am encouraging those of a more traditional minded way of spirituality to read this book is because it holds much truth from enlightened beings Whether or not this information is 100% accurate *(as this information did not come directly to me)* I feel I am discerning enough to know that the messages of Love in this book...becoming one with our Source our God Self, is vital information at this time on Mother Earth. We can all come into the Light of Pure Love for all Humankind through meditation practice and Love, as we are all spiritual beings living what appears to be a human experience.

Whether one believes that great changes are about to happen here or not does not mean that it is not going to happen and that great change has already begun. The veil is getting thinner and more portals to higher dimensions are opening. If we are prepared, we can assist ourselves, our families AND our careers to be not only in the light and become empowered but also assist our world. So if you have ever felt that you are alone on your journey then this book may give you some clarity and vision for a new life and a new world. Being prepared for the energy shifts is vital for our finances, our relationships, our inner happiness and it is vital for our beautiful souls purpose to be fulfilled.

In this book you will find so much information covering so many topics that cover the practical and logical to the mystical.

So I will repeat...PLEASE keep an open mind, read and listen with your heart...

In Love and Oneness
Michele
www.MicheleBlood.com

# A WORD FROM ISHTAR

This is not an ordinary book. It is a result of my lifelong exposure to the forces of light and forces of darkness that play the great cosmic drama of liberating this tiny planet. The story begins when I was a child, a 12 year old boy who had no idea what extraordinary turns his life would take. On that night, November 11$^{th}$, I had a dream. In that dream I had a vision of my twin soul and beyond that vision, a Samadhi experience, a moment of enlightenment, a moment of no-time. From that moment on, I knew who I was, who I AM, a search was completed and another one began. A burning desire to liberate this planet. A dedication to start the last revolution, a revolution that will awaken humanity forever. Years later, beings of light, ascended masters, old friends from ages past, contacted me telepathically and transmitted this book to me.

Immediately after the book was published in my home country, the dark forces attacked me physically and energetically. They did not want to destroy my body. They wanted to destroy my soul. And they nearly succeeded. As I had to fight for my life, I gathered all the information I could find about the dark forces. A contact person that was once part of the underground resistance movement assisted me with guidance and actually saved my life. A bigger picture began to emerge and I could see a great cosmic drama unfolding on this planet. As the situation improved, I got into telepathic contact with the Pleiadians, a sister race that has been helping humanity for millennia. They gave me further information that you can find in this book. Now, as my being is becoming pure light, I can see a dawning of a new age for all humanity, Aurora 2012.

Here I would like to give credit to Aristid Havlicek for 'Merkaba Technology' and to Alice A. Bailey for her contribution to the world with 'Triangles Meditation' and with Great invocation, both mentioned in this book. And of course to Helena Petrovna Blavatsky who brought awareness of the ascended masters to humanity.

My thanks and deep appreciation goes to all beings of light, all cosmic races and civilizations of light, all ascended masters and angels. My love goes to all Goddesses that I met or I will meet along my journey, healing places and dimensions within my being, sharing love, joy and oneness. Finally I dedicate this book to my beloved twin soul, to my soulmates and to my soul family.

Ishtar

# ABOUT THE AUTHOR

Ishtar Antares

Ishtar Antares was born in 1971 in Ljubljana, Slovenia. Since childhood he had many spontaneous kundalini experiences that brought to him clear uninterrupted memories of his past incarnations and his existence before he came to this planet in Atlantis. He began conscious channeling in 1993 and started at that time an Ascension group in the capital city of his own country, Slovenia. The power of his message soon reached many people and he was invited by many radio and TV stations in Slovenia to give interviews. He appeared on national TV with almost half of Slovenia watching and listening to his transformative message. His media appearances included Slovenia, Croatia and Italy. He wrote dozens of articles for seven different daily, weekly and monthly magazines.

He gives many workshops on The Ascension Process, Galactic Tantra and The Manifestation Process and Light body activation in Slovenia, Croatia, Hungary, Germany, Czech Republic, Ireland, USA, Australia, Costa Rica and Central America. His book "Ascension Star" was published in Slovenia with great success. Now you are reading an expanded and improved version of that book.

Ishtar Antares lives and works in Slovenia as a Cosmic Astrology consultant. He developed a tachionization chamber and his company "New Energy Tachyon" distributes tachionized products worldwide. He travels worldwide year round, activating sacred spots throughout the planet and spreading his knowledge at live events to those that wish to receive it.

**www.Aurora2012.net**
**to contact Ishtar directly e-mail him at**
**antarion@volja.net**

# PREFACE

**The first part** of this book is a collection of cosmic communications which were given by the Krotron StarBase and mother-ship Excalibur of the Ashtar Command between 1993 and 1995. As in any communication also in these it is not possible to attain perfect reliability of the transmission, therefore it is good for you to check the verity of this information in your heart. At the beginning there is an interview of the author as to certain important questions.

**The second part** of this book is a summary of instructions for creation of living mandalas. It was written between 1996 and 1997. It can be used as a manual for creation of a real living Mandala.

**The third part** of this book was written in 2002, 2003 and later as a result of telepathic contact with Ranutarian division of the Pleiadian fleet within the Galactic Confederation. Part of information was received from a physical contact person that was once part of the Resistance movement. Small fragment of data was received from other sources also.

Soulmates and members of my soul family that feel connected with the vision of manifesting a living Mandala and an Island of Light can reach me at antarion@volja.net . I will also use this opportunity to say thanks to all beings of light that carry on with their missions with utmost dedication of their souls, minds and bodies. www.Aurora2012.net

# CHAPTER ONE

## TRANSITION INTO AQUARIAN AGE

Information about the evacuation of mankind has raised a lot of interest. Let's look at this information from a higher perspective of a transition into a New Age. A change that is now occurring on Earth is only a reflection of a drastic change which is happening on a cosmic scale. There is an alignment of the whole Universe with the will of the Creator and his will is Oneness of the whole creation. So this Universe is responding on impulse from above and changes its state from expansion (out breath) into contraction (in breath).

Now it is exactly in the turning point, in a state of no breath. In this point Divine will can manifest directly through the whole Creation. This energy is transmitted through the centre of the Galaxy in spiral movements outwards. Because of distortions in the space-time continuum structure, it does not reach the whole Galaxy exactly at the same moment of our linear time. Now it has reached our planet and enables us to raise our consciousness from duality into Oneness. Earth is traveling through a ring of Light, which represents the transition zone between old and new energies.

### 11: 11

Zone of ring of Light is an area of dimensional opening of the 11: 11, zone of leap from 3rd to 5th dimension. Entrance in this dimensional opening of the 11: 11 began on the 11th of January 1992 and announced the beginning of rifts in the time-space structure, through which at that date on this planet the energy of cosmic love and oneness began to pour in.

On Earth, the transition in consciousness of Oneness will be taking place in islands of Light. These New Age communities began to be established in 1995. Soul families will gather in those communities, these are groups of people who are aligned as souls. Also soul mates will meet there and twin souls also. Intimate relationships which were in the world of duality possible only between two individuals will expand to a whole group.

On the 11th of August in 1999 at 11 hours 11 minutes at total solar eclipse Earth went through sipapu, a dimensional axis of oneness. This represents a culmination point of transition through the opening of 11:11, where the point of cosmic no breath will reach this planet. The transition through the opening the 11:11 will be continuing on Earth until 2012, when Earth will be accepted in the Galactic network of Lights as an equal Planet.

## THE FIRST WAVE OF ASCENSION

During the transition through the 11:11, Earth is assisted by cosmic brothers, members of the Ashtar Command. This is a large group of about 10 million beings of Light who surround our planet in their space ships. They are guided by Christ or as they call him, Sananda. Currently the first wave of Ascension is in the centre of their attention. Ascension is a rising of consciousness from third dimensional consciousness of duality, where time, space, limitations, causes and consequences, life and death exist into the fifth dimensional consciousness where only light, oneness, love and immortality exist. It is a rising of consciousness into a liberated state of Ascended Masters, which will return later on Earth and create miracles like Jesus did. The first wave of Ascension will happen, when our cosmic brothers will gather among humanity from 1000 - 2000 volunteers which will be ready to give themselves to this process. This will occur with assistance of etheric technology of the liquid light which the Ashtar Command has at its disposal, with activating soul codes which transform our consciousness into the consciousness of the Ascended Master. At the first wave of Ascension the most aware STAR PEOPLE, who live among humanity, will go. STAR PEOPLE are angelic beings which entered human evolution from other star systems, like Sirius or Pleiades. Ascension is for them a logical step in their development. Ascension is a lifting of consciousness, which will be occurring along with a lifting of physical bodies in the space ships with the help of a light beam.

A candidate for Ascension will see then a light opening which will be so intense that he would see it with his eyes open or closed. If he enters this opening he will be lifted on a ship, if he does not he will stay on the Earth. Ascension is actually the free will of individual. By deciding for Ascension we do not need to worry what will happen with the children, because children of Ascended volunteers will go with them. Those volunteers could return later on Earth as Ascended Masters and prepare people for the second wave of Ascension, and lift their consciousness.

The first wave of Ascension is available for everybody; the most important is a sincere and clear decision. Of course, everybody who decides for this will go through the intense and extensive preparations. Those who will not succeed to be prepared at the time of the first Ascension will be most likely prepared in the time of the second wave. Nobody needs to be afraid that he will not make it. It is not important for the Ascension to be completely aware and cleansed. Unconditional decision is much more important. When we accept this decision, our life begins to change extremely fast. A process of cleansing emotional blockades and mental patterns is started. It is important that we do not identify ourselves with the process, that we have our goal always ahead of us and that we trust because this process is guided from above by the Ascended Masters. Regular meditation helps very much. It is good that we forgive ourselves and others, that we release attachments to people, things and situations in our lives and that we clear all unfinished. Then we can open our heart towards beauty and raise our consciousness.

## THE SECOND WAVE OF ASCENSION

When the Masters who will return to Earth after the first wave will gather enough volunteers, the second wave of Ascension will take place. There are about 144.000 of volunteers needed for the second wave. This is a critical mass of Ascended Masters, which is needed for the humanity as a whole, to go into the New Age. When the Masters of the second wave return to Earth, they will prepare people for the third wave and evacuation.

## THE THIRD WAVE OF ASCENSION AND EVACUATION

The third wave of evacuation will happen around the time of evacuation of mankind. As long as the evacuation is only a lifting of physical body into the space ship, the Ascension represents also a lifting of consciousness.

All people will be informed about evacuation in the right time, through the media or through telepathic communication, and evacuation will be available for everybody. The sky will be covered by large mother-ships and there from the smaller ships will descend right until the surface of Earth, and those smaller ships will emanate a special light beam. Everybody, who would, by his free decision, enter that light beam, would be evacuated. Evacuation will be taking place very fast, about 15 minutes for all mankind. It will be most important at that time that people will trust ships, that they will not be afraid.

Unattachment towards material things is also important, because when we will go upon the ships we will not take anything with us. Upon the ships people will gather together and find their families and friends. Then they will have an opportunity for choice. If they would like to live in duality as before on

Earth, they will be evacuated on other planets. If they would like to live as beings of Light, they could return to Earth as Ascended Masters. In the meantime Earth will become a Planet of Light. Those who are STAR PEOPLE could return to home planets or go to higher level of being, or, of course, they could also stay on Earth.

# MERGER

Beloved family of starry angels has activated inner fire in our rainbow bodies and began to gather in vortices of deliverance to build together the Galactic network of light. The spark of our divine will has begun to create energetic vortices that call other parts of our starry being and then merged together as cosmic mother-father we create twelve fold stars of Ascension...

We are in time of sacred union. We are in a time of group intimacy. Intimacy is that which brings us closer together: telling deeper truth about ourselves, expressing our feelings, merging physically. Experiencing all energies through our heart in a group. Merging of soul families with our bodies and souls. Everybody can join and is accepted. But there needs to be a yearning for Oneness in our hearts, openness on all levels and willingness to release all possessiveness and to release all relationships that do not bring us happiness.

In our groups we meet each other as angel beings and men and women simultaneously. We heal the split between our love energy and our sexual energy. We express our sexual energy through our open heart and fuse it with energy of love. Many times we do not need to express it in a sexual union. Many times it is enough that we express it with a gentle touch. And it will transform into love and create a fifth dimensional field of liquid light.

We deepen our sacred union with deep sixth dimensional soul mate relationships and by becoming One being with our beloved twin soul in octave seven. These new relationships are external manifestation of our light body. They enable the manifestation of fifth- to seventh- dimensional reality in physical world. All beings that merge with us are multidimensional projections of One divine spark, scattered fragments of starry being that now merge into One being again.

All these multidimensional interlocking levels of merger create wheels within wheels of spiral movements that create the vortex of Ascension. This vortex serves as a multidimensional buffer during our transition from third to seventh dimension (octave seven). It causes the activation of group light body and finally group Ascension.

# WHERE ARE WE GOING?

Hello, dear brothers and sisters. This is the Ashtar Command, Krotron Star Base. We are your cosmic brothers; we are coming in peace and Light to help you in this transition in a new state of consciousness. Your world is amidst great changes and is on a brink of a great evolutionary leap. Your world will be taken into the Light. Rejoice because the time of deliverance has come.

## S A N A N D A

In our light ships we encircle your Planet and the one that you call Christ and we call Orthon Sananda is guiding us. And in his name we are giving you a message of redemption. Redemption on your world will happen in three waves of Ascension. And now we are issuing a call to those among you who would like to be ascended in the first wave .Those who will decide for that will be lifted on our the space ships by the use of the light column and upon our ships a transformation of your consciousness will be taking place. Your consciousness will be expanded from the third dimensional human consciousness into infinite fifth dimensional consciousness, which will expand beyond all spaces and times into no-time and no-space. You will realize joy of liberated being; you will live in cosmic love. Your mortal body will transform into eternal body of Light that you will be like Angels in Heaven.

Then you could return to Earth, walk among your human brothers and sisters and spread the presence of Love. You will gather in Communities of Light and show people the path of Light in line with the natural laws. But your return to Earth is not the only choice. You could travel further in depths of space and explore miraculous worlds.

Know that the final time has come, that we have been waiting for thousands of years. Now all yearnings of all hearts will be completed, miracles of all miracles will happen. Miracles are natural expression of Love in cosmos, only on your planet you believe otherwise.

If there is a yearning for deliverance in your heart, if there is a yearning to become a being of Light in your heart, make your decision. The Ascension process is a transformation which is available for everybody, who decides for that. When you accept this decision we will begin to help you on this path by sending you the energy of Light and Love. Cleansing of your thoughts, feelings and bodies will start to prepare you for extremely high vibration of Light beam which will pull you upon the ships. Your perception of world and life will begin to change. Rigid thought patterns will begin to fall apart and will make room for the presence of Love. Suppressed emotions of anger, fear or sadness will begin to surface that you would make them conscious and release them. Everything which was hidden will become visible, to be healed with love. Your body will react on higher vibration with different unusual symptoms. Sometimes you will be tired or sleepy without any obvious reason, sometimes exceptionally full of energy.

## PATH INTO UNKNOWN

If you decide for the Ascension this is a path to unknown. Therefore it is important to listen to the wisdom of your heart, which knows what is true, which knows that the Ascension is a path of Love. Doubts and tests will appear. If you would like to enter into the Ascended state, it is important to release all the attachments to your third dimensional world. In one moment you will face the moment of decision between your old and new reality. Then you will know that you need to release everything, which is not in the resonance with your highest truth, but you need to release all compromises, if you would like to go ahead. Then go deeper in your heart where you will find peace and insist at your decision. Open to our presence, call us, invite us in your life. Many people in your country are already connecting with us and are receiving many gifts from us. There is no reason for you not being among them.

It is important for you to learn self-love. Forgive yourself all debts that you might have, because you are a beautiful Divine being. And when you forgive yourself, your heart will open and you will forgive your brothers and sisters. Focus upon that which is true and search for beauty everywhere you go. Beauty will lead you in a new world, which soon will be everything which exists, because the former world will fall apart.

The first wave of Ascension will happen in a moment, when there are enough volunteers all around the world. This could be at any moment. So be awake and ready. When that moment comes we will overflow you with Light, so that you will see pillar of Light clearly in front of you, with your eyes open or closed. And if you enter this pillar we will take you upon the ships. By this decision do not worry what will be with your closest that you leave behind. They will be taken care of. If you have children they will go along with you. All the others who are close to you will be informed about your departure in their dreams. Actually you will not depart anybody. Mostly you will return to Earth in few months to lead all humanity into the Light. And we are with you...

# A CALL TO THE STARRY FAMILY

We are your brothers and sisters of light; we are here with you to issue a call of awakening. It has come a time for you to awaken and radiate in your light bodies as angelic beings and prepare for your Ascension.

Once long ago in the past the whole starry family was living in a beautiful oneness. You have entered duality to gain wisdom and now you can enter even greater oneness. Transition from duality into oneness is occurring right now. Between 1992 and 2011 your planet is traveling through the dimensional doorway of 11:11, a ring of light that is a band of energy of a very high vibration. It is a zone of overlap between two very different systems of evolution, that of duality and that of oneness. During this time whole star family will ascend, merge with cosmic brotherhood and then return through the star gate of AN in Orion into galactic evolution of oneness. Together we will build a galactic network of light. And now we are issuing a call to your awakening and uniting of starry family on this planet, so we can all together go home, into galactic oneness.

Your awakening begins, when you realize that you are angel coming from the stars. You begin to feel your angelic beauty; you are becoming aware that you are omnipresent One consciousness. You are existing in a zone of no-time in eternal now. So you are entering a new world, a world of oneness...

As a starry being you are emanating a magnetic vortex of angelic energies that call your soul family, your soul mates and twin soul. You will create new forms of relating with them. Old perception of duality which allows only two beings to be intimately together will be greatly expanded. Many of you will form a group, unite and merge in sacred intimate oneness. And you will be close to each other as you were close when you were dolphins in the star system of Sirius.

We are issuing a call to you to create groups, where you will meet each other as souls, as angelic beings of light. There you will support each other. Healing of relationships will take place. Finally you will allow yourselves to be what you are and express your inner beauty. And when you will see beauty in each other you will open your hearts. Belief patterns will be replaced by spontaneity; jealousy, dependence and possessiveness will fall away into nothingness. You will experience a living presence and your yearnings will be met by fulfilling oneness. In those groups many taboos regarding physical touch and expression of sexual energy will be transcended. You will express this energy with an open heart and this will allow healing to take place. You will learn to be together as men and women and star angels simultaneously. Nurture each other, touch each other, kiss each other, merge together, let love flow, dear angels.

Call your soul mates and twin souls, create deep relationships with them. Connect with all of them in a small intimate group. You will feel deep understanding and alignment with those beautiful souls. You will meet your ideal mate, your twin soul. You will merge with her into one being. All this will accelerate your path dramatically, you will begin your group Ascension process and begin to enter etheric spiral of oneness that is invisible to your physical eyes.

World of duality and world of oneness are two worlds, each with its own natural laws. They are not compatible. You can not live in both worlds simultaneously. At some point you need to make a decision for one or the other. No compromise. If you decide for world of oneness, release all relationships that do not bring you happiness, that do not bring you joy, but suffering. You do not need to learn through suffering anymore. You are light beings and you will learn through love, through loving relationships. You are guardians of oneness for this planet, so take care for your happiness.

Spiritual groups of soul families, soul mates and twin souls are coming together all around the world in rainbow vortices of Ascension to fulfill the last task - Ascension of your planet. In your world there are many spiritual groups that have the same purpose, but sometimes they are not aware of it.

Purpose of every true spiritual group is ultimate liberation of man, his Ascension. And now there is a great need for synthesis of all points of light, all spiritual groups no matter what their outer form, to create together a network of light. Through this network you will radiate light and love as one being. And love will flow around your world and heal wounded humanity. And in this sacred task, we are with you....

# EVACUATION: PATH INTO THE LIGHT

This is the Ashtar Command. We are here to encourage you and to assure you that there is no reason for fear. The change that is intended for this planet is already happening and will reach its climax in transformation of the Earth surface. A great quantity of Light and Love will be present at that moment. Don't look at that as a cataclysm but rather as a path into the Light.

## EVERYBODY WILL HAVE FREE CHOICE

We will rescue every human being, who will decide for that by his free will. We will carry people to various planets, regarding their own choice and degree of their development that they will be among equals. If anybody would like to live in a world of duality, we will carry him to a planet, where he could live like that. There he will have the opportunity to develop inside his own chosen reality in much better circumstances than here on Earth, but he will still be, to some expand, subject to his emotions and emotions of people around him, who will choose the same reality. They will live similarly as here on Earth, but without wars, famine and natural disasters. They will have an opportunity to learn to live together more peacefully as before on Earth. Those who will, instead of duality, rather choose Oneness, will have an opportunity to return to Earth, as Ascended Masters and live in a New Age in perfect happiness. Some people, who are actually STAR PEOPLE, will choose return to their home planets. Some of them will choose a journey in higher dimensions beyond the unknown. Everybody will decide by his freewill, nobody will be punished, because all people are innocent sons and daughters of God. And innocence of soul in a heart of every human is a guarantee for everybody who wants to ascend into the Light. But many will choose otherwise, which is all right, because everybody will accept choices which are most suitable for him.

Only ones who will need to die will be those representatives of Dark Forces, who do not wish to stop spreading the negativity. But nobody of you is among them, so do not worry.

## WE ARE LIVING IN EXTRAORDINARY TIMES

Around your planet there is a great presence of Light, many Angelic beings and Masters of Wisdom. They are directing this energy of Light to human beings who can use that Light in their spiritual development. So you would do a very good thing for yourself if you would open for this manifestation of Light and if you would open your hearts towards each other. Forgive yourself and each other because you are all innocent beings. You are all beautiful beings. You are not just small humans with everyday problems; you are much more than that. You are immortal Beings of Light. Awake to this reality, discover who you are actually, and try to bring in your life that which is eternal, that which uplifts you. And search for beauty in your life's and spread it around. You do not need to wait for an evacuation or transformation of Earth, this will all come at the right time, so do not worry. You will all be informed and ready enough when the time comes. Until then live your life in its fullness. Enjoy in your life, try to fill it with rainbow, which is inside of you and try to connect with us. We are always willing to connect with you in all possible ways. Try to reach us in your meditations. We can help you a lot, even in your physical life. You would be very surprised if you would know how much help you can get from Ascended Masters. We are not working only with groups. Each individual human being is important to us. We would like to stress again that there is a lot of Love present around your Planet. You can call that Love; focus your attention on it. If you would like to complete your cycle of embodiments as human being and live as Ascended Master, this is available for you. This is called the Ascension. Yes, you can experience the Ascension in this lifetime, but you need to wish that. We send you our blessings. This is the Ashtar Command.

## MEDITATION FOR CONNECTION WITH ASHTAR COMMAND

Relax yourself, close your eyes and watch your breath. Imagine that you are surrounded and protected with a brilliant white Light. Watch your breath which comes and goes and this will relax you. Then watch your feelings and then your thoughts for a minute. Think about the Ashtar Command and call for connection with your entire mind, with all of your being. Focus your attention towards your heart centre, breath through it and be open for connection. A connection which comes is always very gentle, full of Light. It is never sudden. If thoughts appear just return your consciousness towards breathing through the heart centre. And through some time you will begin to receive telepathic messages.

# LET US BECOME MASTERS OF WISDOM

We are amidst extraordinary times. In time that this world has not seen it yet. In times when we can accelerate our spiritual development dramatically, achieve mastery over our human life, ascend and become Masters of Wisdom.

Hello, brothers and sisters. This is the Ashtar Command. We are here to represent to you the greatest adventure in your life. This adventure is your spiritual path towards your liberation, towards y our mastery, towards your final liberation. This is your ultimate heritage, your ultimate goal. What is the Ascension? This is your liberation from the world of duality, when you know finally who you really are, this is life eternal, full of joy and fulfillment. Your consciousness will be expanded more than you have ever dreamed. You will be liberated from all karma and manifestations of the world of duality. You will become Masters of Wisdom. You will have immortal youthful bodies, if you would like to manifest in your physical body. You will have the power of manifesting whatever you wish but your purpose will be always aligned with the Divine Plan. You could heal, teach humanity, do a lot of good.

## THREE WAVES

This transformation is not intended for certain chosen individuals. It is available for everybody who has an open heart and wishes to live a higher truth. This is the major requirement for the Ascension process. Therefore we will try to clear this process somewhat to make yourself decide easier. Do you like to ascend or not? The ascension path is gradual path with culmination in the final event. The final event is actual

Ascension. There will be three waves of Ascension: the first one will be the lifting of the most conscious STAR PEOPLE (beings who have incarnated among humanity from other Star systems) in their true state, the second will be lifting of other STAR PEOPLE in ascended state, and the third will be the Ascension of that part of humanity which will be open for this process. Let us clear that evacuation and Ascension are two different things. Evacuation is lifting of your bodies in etheric space ships, while the Ascension is lifting of your consciousness from the third dimensional space-time in the fifth dimensional consciousness of Oneness, Love and Light. Ashtar Command has spiritual technology of love, admitted to a disposal, which can dramatically accelerate your growth. The first wave is right ahead of us, it can happen any time. This is just an estimate because the exact date is not known. The second wave will occur soon after the first one and the third one will be at the evacuation of mankind.

## HOW IT WILL HAPPEN?

At the time of Ascension, few hours before the actual lifting, you will feel around yourself a lot of Love and Light, Clarity and Peace; you will feel our presence intensively. Then you will have an opportunity to release your attachments towards the world of duality for the last time and to make your final decision about the Ascension. Then a column of Light will appear in front of you and you could see it with your eyes open or closed. You will receive guidance and you will know spontaneously what to do. If you enter this Light column you will be taken to the ships. With your guidance you will be, before that moment, and after that but in the exact moment you will be on your own, because the decision for the Ascension will be accepted by your freewill. Those of you who would feel unpleasantly upon our space ship will be taken into a surrounding which will suit you better. There you will have time to rest and then you will experience the actual Ascension of consciousness. After that you will have an opportunity for choice. You could stay upon the ships, you could choose to go in higher dimensions of consciousness or you could choose to return on Earth as an Ascended Master. At this time there is a great need for Ascended Masters. As an Ascended Master you could do a lot of good in building New Age, in healing and lifting the consciousness of people. And many Masters will return. They could perform their Divine missions much more effectively than before when they were still, to some extent, subject to the world of duality. The Ascension process requires quite a lot of preparations, working on yourself, especially for healing of emotional body.

# PREPARATIONS FOR THE ASCENSION

The Ascension path is very intense one, because in a very short time a great shift of consciousness is created. This requires a lot of work for your own spiritual growth. And it brings also a lot of joy...

Hello, dear Beings of Light. This is the Ashtar Command. We will speak this time about the preparations for the Ascension, because the Ascension is a process to which you dedicate your whole life. Our wish is that as many beings as possible will get this information that their purpose in this lifetime is to graduate from Earth School of Spirituality and become a Master of Wisdom.

But there is also a certain danger in spreading this information. We see that many of you are quite excited when you hear those messages. This we understand. But there is a tendency in some of you to wait for the ships for deliverance and forget about your life here. This we do not recommend. We recommend you that you accept a firm decision for the Ascension inside of you, walk along your path with trust and cooperate with us in your spiritual growth. We also wish that you are not overly attached to the information we are giving you, simply listen to yourself and know that you will be ascended if this is your decision and remain responsible. You are responsible for your life here, for your growth so accept responsibility and your life will become better. You do not need to have complete intellectual understanding for your Ascension. It is also not needed for you to become perfect spiritual humans.

Your firm decision and openness of your heart is much more important. Regarding intellectual understanding: your mental body is receiving needed instructions while you sleep on our ships. Therefore you will know exactly what to do when the time comes.

## MIRACLE OF SELF LOVE

It is very important that you love yourself, regardless of everything. Take your time to be gentle with yourself, because true healing comes only through self love.

Many need love desperately. Turn inwards, open your heart and experience the beauty of your soul. It would be very useful if you could meditate every day. This is almost a requirement if you wish to ascend. Because meditation brings you closer to your soul, which is a source of the self love. Release all feelings of unworthiness and guilt. You do not need them any more. All that you have done is forgiven. Do not be afraid to ask for love, if you need it. Be like children, we will help you, we will guide you towards love inside and outside of yourselves. If you would like we can send you love through your heart centre. Love is energy and we can direct it towards you and if you are open enough you can accept it. Benefit of increased self love is that you can share it with others. And when you give you accept even more. This is a miracle of bathing in the sea of Love.

## THE COURSE OF TRANSFORMATION

The transformation that you are going into is enormous. It surely involves a lot of emotional cleansing. You will come face to face with emotional processes; you will release feelings of fear, anger, sadness... This does not mean that you need to sink into them but you release them; you will expand your consciousness beyond them. And try to do that as gently as possible, because those processes could sometimes be very intense. Keep your faith and trust and do not identify too much with them. Focus upon the positive. Your mental body is also changing. You are going beyond your old memories, old patterns, and old ways of perception. Do not hold on to them but release them. That what is ahead of you is much bigger. Sometimes you will doubt or be confused. This is just a part of the process. Try to meditate then, to connect with us. Ask us for help. Even your physical body is responding on increased inflow of energy. Sometimes you will have strange feelings in your bodies, you will hear strange voices, and you will sleep a lot or almost nothing and many other things. May this not confuse you. Nurse your body, give it food and enough relaxation, movement, and above all, Love.

It is important for you to release your attachment towards the world of duality. You can do that on your own way, but it would be good to call us to assist you with that. You can call Archangel Michael, who is an expert for releasing attachment to this world. Also you need to clear all unfinished issues in your life.

Release everything which is not in resonance with your highest truth. What will remain is Light, Truth and Love. And this will fill your life. Some of you are worried what will happen with your fellowmen whom you will leave behind upon your Ascension. Do not worry. They will be taken care of. If you have children who are not able to sustain themselves they will go along with you. We send you Love and Light. This was the Ashtar Command.

# 11: 11

11: 11 is a dimensional cosmic doorway which leads into oneness. Let us go through it.

Hello, brothers and sisters. This is the Ashtar Command. This time we will speak about the greatest transition between two various reality systems which has ever happened. Let us say, that the whole Universe is in a state of drastic reorganization. It is aligning itself with the will of Creator and his will is oneness of all the Creation. So this Universe is now responding on impulse from above and changes its state from expansion (out breath) into contraction (in breath). Now it is exactly in a turning point, in a state of no-breath. In this point the Divine will could manifest directly through whole Creation. This energy is transmitted through Galactic Central Sun and then throughout the Galaxy in spiral movements outwards. Because of distortions in space-time structure it does not reach the whole Galaxy at the same moment of the linear time. And now it has reached your Planet and enables you to change your reality system from duality into oneness.

This is the dimensional doorway, called the 11: 11. This is a doorway of consciousness, which is set free from duality and separation and enters a total oneness. This is available for you. You live in time where all doors are open. So release all ideas about your ability or inability to reach higher spiritual evolution or liberation. You live in time of miracles, so everything is possible. Entering in state of oneness is always in present moment, not in the past and not in the future, so try to live in a present moment. Symbolically speaking, in a state of no-breath. Connect with the Stars and their message of oneness; connect with trees and their message of oneness. Connect with each other and create oneness. Create groups of oneness, communities of oneness, because you are creating a New World.

And what you will believe will be. So try to focus on a new state of consciousness, expand your perspective and insist in your endeavor towards the goal. You can not miss. Oneness is intended for you, it is your deepest essence. And in these times you can not escape from that. Trust life which will guide you with its lessons closer and closer to that what you really are and you are the oneness.

## THE 11: 11 DOORWAY

Dimensional doorway of the 11: 11 was activated on this Planet by masses of STAR PEOPLE on the 11th of January 1992. It will remain open until the 11th of November 2011. During this time your Planet is traveling through a ring of Light which represents a border between two reality systems, between the world of duality and the world of oneness. This is a border between the area which is already impregnated with the new energy from the Galactic Central Sun and the area which is not yet exposed to this increased presence. Ring of Light is a band of extremely increased energy, which is creating in a merging point between two various reality systems.

During the transition through the ring of Light your evolution is accelerated many hundred times. You will discover that you are traveling from your old reality into a new one. Your perception of time, space and matter is changing. Your perspective is expanding. Focus your consciousness in this new reality, because for some time you will live in both realities simultaneously and with a dramatic speed you will transit from one into the other. By focusing into the higher, in what is eternal, you can make this transition easier for yourself. So give your hands to each other and give your hands to us, because we are all one. This is the Ashtar Command. Greetings.

# STAR PEOPLE

We are here to awaken. We are here to manifest sacred dreams. We are here to become Light Eternal. We are STAR PEOPLE. ..

Dear brothers and sisters, Hello. This is the Ashtar Command. This time we are here to remind you who you really are and where are you coming from. Probably you have been asking yourselves many times. And now, in these glorious times, answers are flowing to your hearts like water of life.

## WHERE ARE YOU FROM?

There was time, before you came to Earth, time of infinite joy. You were great Angelic beings, you lived your beautiful life's in Ascended state, like one always connected with the oneness of Creation. But then a call has come throughout the Universe, a call from Planet Earth, which needed volunteers to help her. A great drama was taking place on Earth. A new race was created - humanity. And young, inexperienced human race needed assistance from more developed beings by its development. Many of you have answered that call.

Angelic beings from the Pleiades, those from Sirius and Aldebaran, even some space beings from our sister Galaxy in Andromeda.

## WHY ARE YOU HERE?

And you have gathered together around this beautiful Earth in cosmic ships, in cities of Light, and created together the Ashtar Command. Many beings of the Ashtar Command have never incarnated on Earth. Others did and these are you. If you read these lines with interest and they touch your heart it is a very strong sign, that you are a STAR PERSON and a member of the Ashtar Command. Many Star Beings have incarnated many times on Earth and helped humanity. As a whole you have accelerated evolution of mankind dramatically. But your existence in third dimensional world acted as an anesthetic on your consciousness, you have forgotten who you were and where were you coming from. Most of you have slipped into unconscious state. Now many of you are awakening and this gives us hope and actually enables the process of Ascension to occur on this planet. This planet serves as some kind of acupunctural point which causes transformation and healing of huge parts of Galaxy. And when Earth will be Ascended, Light and Love will spread from here throughout the Galaxy. There are many more planets which are becoming Love and Light right now and you will have the opportunity to visit them after the Ascension.

## STAR CHILDREN

Some of you have spent most of your evolution outside Planet Earth. In space ships you have traveled throughout the Universe. You have incarnated on Earth just a few times. You are the STAR CHILDREN. In this life you have most likely felt alienated from third dimensional world and had great inner knowing about your Star origin. Maybe you were thinking that you were not quite normal or even that you were mad. Nothing could be further from truth. You are Light Beings. You have come from Worlds of Light to help heal this wounded humanity. It is not time any more for you to hide, it is time now to speak open about your truth. And what is even more important, to live it. Love yourself just as you are and do not try to live by expectations of others. You can not fulfill those expectations. You can only fulfill your higher purpose. And your higher purpose is to know eternal life that you can give to others. If people are judging your Angelic presence, forgive them and continue on your path firmly. You are what you are. You do not need to apologize to anybody that you are Star Beings. Invoke your Angelic self, your Angelic presence. You feel it in your meditations, in your every day's life. Ask your Angelic self to give you your Star Name. This is your true name, which is eternal. Use it. You do not need to limit yourselves any more. Try to live as Angelic Being and try to bring Angelic Light into this world. This world is hungry for Light and each of you has a unique contribution in spreading the Light. Connect with us; connect with Angels around you, those in human bodies and those without them. You are not alone though you feel sometimes like that. You have many friends. You have each other. Trees, flowers, animals, are your friends. Dolphins are your friends especially. They are also Star Beings. They come from Sirius. They know how to love. And if you think that you have forgotten how to love, connect with them in your meditation, in your heart. This was the Ashtar Command. Blessings to you all. El-iona-oja-him.

# YOUR DIVINE MISSION

Each of you has a Divine mission on this world, which can not be done by anybody else. Each of Star Beings has a dream about Heaven on Earth, which we will now manifest into reality.

Greetings, dear Angels of Light. This is the Ashtar Command. We shall speak about one of the most important things in the world which will become even more important as you grow; it is your divine mission. Mostly all of you, who are reading this, are Star Beings. Most of you feel that you are on this planet with a certain mission. All of you have some kind of ideal, some dreams. Manifesting your dreams is a part of your Divine mission, because one of the reasons why there are so many STAR PEOPLE on Earth is to create Heavenly world in matter, so Heaven and Earth can come together and merge in one. By nurturing your dreams and doing everything what is in your power to manifest them, you are actually carrying out your Divine mission. You always receive instructions for your next step, from your inner voice. Inner voice is always speaking to you, if you calm down and you are willing to listen to it. And then act accordingly. Many of you wish to know what is your mission that is intended for you, because you feel you are not doing what you came here for. There is a reason for that and this is that most of you can carry out the Divine missions only in new spiral of evolution, in a world of Oneness. In a world of duality you can not manifest Heaven on Earth. This is the reason why many of your efforts in manifesting your ideals have not had the desired results. Manifesting of your dreams is coming closer and is on its way. Be patient and insist and trust. It will happen when you will be centered in oneness enough. Some of you feel caught in jobs, which you feel that are not aligned with your higher purpose. Be aware that you have chosen them yourself. One of the things that you can do is to bring more of a higher purpose in work that you are doing for your survival. Other possibility is that you get engaged in activities which are more aligned with that what you are, with your purpose.

It can be a hobby at the beginning, but this hobby will most likely replace your former job. Currently there are many changes and alignments on this area among STAR PEOPLE. Your Divine mission is not only a certain activity; your purpose is being what you are, being a Star Angel and spreading your presence. And your presence is Love, Truth and Healing. And when you do that there are many opportunities appearing, there are new possibilities revealing themselves which will transform your life beautifully. Just being is enough. Simply being, taking your time to experience the beauty of your inner being and spreading this beauty around. This is the most effective help that you can offer to this planet which needs healing so much.

## SPIRITUALIZATION OF MATTER

The core of your mission is spiritualization of matter of your bodies, your physical, emotional and mental bodies and activation of your Light body which is the carrier of your Angelic self. That means that you will purify the matter, which creates your bodies to that extent that your personality will become a way of expression for your Angelic self. This is a process of self healing, which will result in personal happiness and fulfillment. And when enough beings go through this transformation, waves of happiness and fulfillment will spread around the planet and cause massive quantum leap of consciousness. And this is a process of Ascension culminating in actual lifting in a consciousness of Ascended Masters. This will happen in three waves, as a result of interactions between you and us. Of course, Ascension is not the final step in this transformation. It is only one step on a way through the 11: 11, which is a doorway of consciousness of total oneness.

Traveling through 11: 11 continues in even higher states of consciousness, which you will experience after your

Ascension. Then you will be centered firmly in your Oneness and free in discovering higher areas. Some of you will do that on new Earth and help birthing the new World, others will travel further in new Heaven. Each of you has choices ahead and each of you will choose in alignment with your inner truth. If Oneness is your decision, do not wait for Ascension to bring it to you. Begin living in Oneness now. Don't forget that from the 11th of January 1992 the 11:11 is open wide and you can enter.

Begin living oneness and Ascension will be your next step, which will lead you beyond all boundaries into unknown. Be in the Light.

The Ashtar Command is sending greetings to you.

# RELATIONSHIPS AMONG YOU

Beloved Family of Starry Angels has activated inner fire in our rainbow bodies and began to gather in vortices of redemption to build together the Galactic network of Light.

The spark of our Divine will has begun to create energetic vortices that call other parts of our Starry being and then merge together as Cosmic Mother-Father and we create twelve fold Stars of Ascension.

This is the Ashtar Command, Krotron Star Base, Ixataar intercept 11:11:83. Today we shall speak about your personal relationships. Many of you are in a state of transition between two worlds. You are raising your consciousness from the third dimensional world of duality into experiencing oneness, into merger of Heaven and Earth.

During this transition all of your relationships are changing dramatically. There is a great need for creating relationships on a totally new basis on this world. Many of you, who are on spiritual path, are inclined towards creating relationships on a basis of spiritual laws, that you have accepted inside yourselves and try to live in accordance with them. This could be tricky, because human mind is interpreting spiritual laws by its own and is inclined towards blocking spontaneity and pure expression of the heart.

Along with that you have accepted many unpleasant experiences in your emotional bodies in the past and you have closed yourself down in order to feel safe and protected. It is understandable, but the transformation, in amidst the which you are, is leading you towards the openness of your heart, towards closeness and intimacy. You do not need to be dependent upon each other; also it is not needed that you are far away from each other. Listen to Love and not to fear. You can be close to each other in many ways. Open your heart completely, release judgments that you have towards each other, be sincere and true towards each other. Be what you are. Don't deny that. You are not responsible how others are seeing you. When you will express that what you are, you will soon discover, that you are surrounded by people that are your kindred souls.

These are your Starry brothers and sisters. In following years you will create communities with them, where you will discover new ways of the commune living.

## INTIMATE GROUP CONSCIOUSNESS

Most of you feel that you can be in an intimate relationship only with one person. This perception needs to be expanded, because there is a true group consciousness emerging which will lead into greater Love and fulfillment in relationships. We are certain that you are all fed up with third dimensional relationships with their endless quarrels and compromises. There is something much more beautiful waiting for you. The Oneness you are entering is transcending compromises.

In a world of Oneness beings with common vision are connecting. And if a group of people is aligned with the truth, there is no need to quarrel because everybody knows his own way which is aligned with a path of the whole. In higher worlds it is always like that. Despite that in this world you have somehow forgotten what is possible and what you can manifest. It is good for you to express your feelings to each other, that you share your experiences. Also be gentle to each other, nurture each other. Touch a lot with each other. This creates feeling of oneness and support. During this transition into the world of Oneness it is good to be an alliance, to trust each other. Be sexually open towards each other. You do not need to block your sexual energy. This is a beautiful energy. In its essence it is the energy of Love. Only your judgment can separate sexuality from Love. In fact they are one. Allow others to be close to you and be close to others. But do not attach too much towards each other. Be deep, but also be open and flexible. Forgive all feelings of jealousy and possessiveness. Do not plan too much for the future. Live for the present moment and be joyful together. Many unexpected and beautiful things will happen in following years so do not limit yourself with your expectations. What will happen is far beyond expectations and wild dreams. You can all relax and be what you are. Drop all masks. You do not need them any more. They belong to the world of duality, which you are leaving now. Speak the truth, but speak it in a way, that does not hurt the others but encourages them. You are so beautiful beings and yet you forget that so often, especially when you are engaged in the interpersonal relationships. Be aware of your inner beauty and share it with others. It is not a time of isolation, now it is a time for a merger, openness and intimacy. Because we are all one. This was the Ashtar Command, Krotron Star Base. We wish that you stay full of Light. Blessings to all.

# TWIN SOULS, SOUL MATES AND SOUL FAMILIES

We are not alone. Beloved souls, which we feel very close are traveling along with us in oneness ...

Hello, dear Masters, dear Beings of Light. This is the Ashtar Command, Krotron Star Base. We shall speak to you about those precious beings, which are especially aligned with you.

## TWIN SOULS

Each Being, which decided to incarnate in the world of matter, needs to do that in combination with the twin soul. This does not mean that a soul splits apart but it incarnates in two bodies. One of them represents feminine and the other one masculine aspect of yourself. Many of you have a wish for ideal love relationship and this wish emerges from connection with your twin soul. Some of you will meet the twin souls before the Ascension. Others will need to wait for the Ascension waves because at this time all twin souls are not incarnated. Be aware that a relationship with the twin soul can not liberate you. Be fulfilled inside of yourself and firmly anchored in a world of Oneness and then the purpose of the love connections between the twin souls will reveal magically to you. Because truly, relationship with the twin soul is a wonderful experience. It creates a double pillar of Light, Love and Oneness for the whole planet. Meetings of twin souls which will be intensively taking place upon the whole world are heralding the completion of duality and entering into the world of Oneness. Some of you are willing to create fulfilling love relationship, and at the same time your twin soul is not incarnated. In this case there is a soul mate, which channels the presence of your twin soul and with that being you can connect in a fulfilling relationship.

## SOUL MATES AND SOUL FAMILIES

Along with the twin souls there are also other souls with which you can create love relationships. These are your soul mates. These are beings of opposite sex which whom you share alignment of inner being and deep understanding. Connect with them. Many soul mates upon the whole Planet would like to connect with you. You have also starry friends, Starry brothers and sisters. You share a common origin with them, common internal characteristics, common yearnings of heart. Together you create a soul family. This is your true family. In the following years more and more soul families will begin to live in Communities of Oneness, in Islands of Light.

## HOW WE MEET EACH OTHER?

You will all meet your twin souls, soul mates and soul families at the right time. The right time will be when you will create relationships with others as souls, as Starry Angelic beings. When you will see others as Starry Angelic beings. To meet your beloved souls you do not need to do anything special, just be. If you feel yearning for merger with them, send it from your heart all around the world. Let it flow. Connect with your beloved souls in your imagination, if you had not met them yet. Imagination is your doorway into Heavenly worlds of the Heaven on Earth. Many of those, that you are yearning for, are on the ships of the Ashtar Command. So connect with us. We shall meet up there ....

ASHTAR COMMAND KROTRON STARBASE
IXATAAR INTERCEPT 11:11:83 END OF TRANSMISSION

---

# ANTARION CONVERSION

Antarian Conversion means completion of duality and transition into the world of Oneness.. Let us see how this transition looks like ...

This is the Ashtar Command, Krotron StarBase. We are here with you to explain to you the transition that is occurring on your world, but not only on your world exclusively, for this is occurring throughout the whole dimensional universe as a result of a new dispensation of divine light of One.

For a long time, this planet was existing and evolving within the dimensional parameters of duality. It was subject to the laws of time and space, cause and effect (sometimes called karma), birth and death, good and evil, the polarities. The evolution of consciousness was achieved through conflicts, through experiencing the opposites, the separation.

Now this world has reached the point where it can graduate from duality and enter a new dimensional patterning of Oneness. This results in drastic changes in consciousness and energy flows which you can already experience. This time of transition and completion is called the Antarion Conversion. The Antarion Conversion is connected with the constellation of Orion which holds the key of duality for this part of the galaxy. There are some very bright and some not so bright beings originating from Orion that are playing major roles in the drama of duality. And planet Earth is currently completing its participation in this drama. For it is entering the world of Oneness, a world of no-time, no-space and no-duality. There will be no more karma, for there will be divine grace flowing, there will be no more death and evil, for it will be transcended by the light of One. This is the time when all judgment will be released as a result of the divine intervention, the energy originating from the One through the Galactic Central Sun system and distributed through many star gates such as Sirius and Alcyone towards this planet. It is changing and transmuting the vibrational frequency of every atom of your planet, every cell of your body.

As a result of this increased energy many star people are awakening upon your planet. Your star codes are being activated. You are gathering together and activating dimensional doorways which allow the Antarion Conversion to occur upon your planet. When enough conscious beings get together with focused intent there is a great amount of this new energy of One that can flow through them. Then this energy flows around the planet and activates the consciousness of many many beings. So a quantum leap is generated.

The first of the major planetary activations was the Harmonic Convergence. It occurred on 16th and 17th August 1987. On that day hundreds of thousands of dedicated beings anchored the fourth dimension, the astral plane, the plane of emotions. Thus access towards the astral plane was much easier and this allowed emotional cleansing on a planetary level. This signifies the beginning of the Antarion Conversion.

## THE 11: 11

The next was the activation of the 11:11 on 11th January 1992. This planetary activation opened the doorway of Oneness. For the first time in the evolution of this planet it was possible to experience the energy of the One directly. The doorway of the 11:11 has eleven gates, which lead directly to Oneness. As the first one was activated on January 11th 1992, the last one will be activated on 11th November 2011. This will be the completion of the Antarion Conversion. Earth will become a heavenly world, originating from the One, living in the subtle currents of cosmic love. It will be a point of light in the Galactic network of light.

The second gate of the 11:11 was activated on 5th June 1993. It was the activation of cosmic love upon this planet. Many of you can feel this increased energy of cosmic love in your life after the second gate activation. This resulted in great changes in your personal relationships. New forms of relating will be created upon your planet and they will lead you even deeper into the light of One.

## THE 12: 12

The shift between the second and the third gate is enormous. So there was another doorway in between, which eased this transition for you. This is the activation of the 12:12. It occurred on 12th December 1994. The main activation was at the great pyramid in Egypt. There was a critical mass of around 1,000-2,000 beings in Egypt and 144,000 worldwide that was necessary for this quantum leap of consciousness to occur. The 12:12 originates from different level of Ascension than the 11:11. The 11:11 is much vaster, leading you to the Galactic Central Sun system. The 12:12 is only one of the dimensional steps in this direction. At this point of transition through the 11:11 all denser levels of duality needed to be completed. So the 12:12 is the last planetary activation within the world of duality and it actually completed your evolution in the denser energies of duality, the energies of judgment. It is linked interdimensionally to the doorway of the 11:11 in terms that it freed you from dense karmic patterns so that you can delve deeper in the subtle energies of the 11:11 and prepared for the activation of the third gate.

It is very important that we explain all these doorways to you. These doorways are a path towards your Ascension. They are allowing the three waves of Ascension to occur. And your Ascension will allow you to delve even deeper into Oneness and continue your transition through the doorway of the 11:11. All these doorways are interdimensional, so they are not easy to be understood with your linear mind. We are understanding this. But however, take some time and effort to study this, for it will give you much insight in your direction in the following years.

So what was the 12:12? It was an interdimensional doorway which was activated by many of you, beloved star brothers and sisters. It was the doorway of completion. It leaded you to the 6th dimensional consciousness of divine grace. This means that your wishes manifest instantly as a result of the expression of your divine being. You begin to be existing in a state of cosmic love. This is available to you; however you still need to stabilize this in your consciousness. The energy of divine grace is emanating through the galactic centre and is transmitted through Sirius by the Great Blue Lodge of Sirius. Our cosmic brothers of the Jupiter Command, which is similar to the Ashtar Command, are directing this energy through Jupiter, which acts as a transformation station that lowers its frequency to the extent that it is usable upon your planet. The comet that struck Jupiter on July 1994 caused energy waves of divine grace that prepared the way for the 12:12. This energy is then gathered and directed by some ascended Masters that form a special group, called the Brotherhood of the Star. This group of Masters is responsible for the completion of duality and for Ascension upon this planet. They are then projecting this energy towards you who are receiving it. It is a very focused, specific ray of energy that allows you to forgive yourself. And self-forgiveness can end the law of karma and establish the law of grace. As a result of this, many of you completed your emotional cleansing before the activation of the 12:12. This allowed you to experience these new energies that reached the Earth on the 12:12 day through the great pyramid and activated your star codes. The 12:12 was a profound shift in your consciousness which allowed the higher star codes of the 11:11 to activate for you. You became ready to receive focused ray of liquid light from us, which stimulated your evolvement. Your evolution was accelerated many, many times.

## THE ANTARION DOORWAY

After the 12:12 activation there came the activation of the third gate of the 11:11, which accelerated things ever further. This created a shift of the mass consciousness of humanity towards the new reality that is miraculously growing upon your planet. It led to the activation of the fourth gate of the 11:11 which is called the Antarion doorway. This was activated on 11th August 1999 at a total solar eclipse, which occurred at 11 hours 11 minutes Greenwich Mean Time. This is the cosmic revelation point that was predicted in your prophecies. It is also the culmination point of transition for this planet. It is the point when cosmic no-breath reached the solar system. For this universe is reaching the exact turning point from expansion to contraction and at this point the light of One can manifest fully throughout the manifested creation.

## THE NEW HEAVEN AND THE NEW EARTH

After the Antarion doorway there are further 11:11 activations, numbering from 5 to 11. They will lead you and us as One in the new reality which is indescribable and is not known even by us. It will allow the vast starry family to travel together as One, beyond the manifested creation, beyond the manifested universes. We are all One.

KROTRON STARBASE
IXATAAR INTERCEPT 11:11:83
END OF
TRANSMISSION

# ASCENSION TIME

Time of great changes is coming. This is a time of completion of the old and birth of the new. Because former world has gone ...

Hello, dear brothers and sisters. This is the Ashtar Command, Krotron Star base. We are with you and you are with us, to rejoice together at the times that are coming. And these are times of deliverance. Through many eons on Earth you were accustomed to the cycle of birth and death, to the reincarnation. And a belief strengthened in yourself that for a perfect spiritual enlightenment a lot of time is needed, a lot of effort, and many lifetimes. You have believed that you have forgotten who you are. And now we are representing you a possibility that you become an Ascended Master in this lifetime. Everybody can achieve that if he decides so. Love of your Divine spark enables you this. Your Divine spark has decided for the Ascension before you had incarnated in this lifetime. How to step on the path of Ascension? Simply, by consciously accepting the decision for the Ascension. Those who would like to go on the first wave decide for that and it is very likely that you will be ready when this happens, because we need a certain number of volunteers for the first wave. The first wave is currently in the centre of our attention and we are collecting volunteers for that.

By deciding for the Ascension you will experience a transformation of consciousness in your life and increase connection with us dramatically. When you are ready you will receive from us an Ascension column. Some of you had already. This is an energetic column which we send from our Star bases and it surrounds your body and increases the vibration of your consciousness. This column is always with you, but you strengthen its effects if you think about it. On the physical plane you can feel its activity as lightness, lifting, as if gravity does not have any hold upon you any more. On the emotional plane you can experience it as an energy of joy and enthusiasm, which permeates your emotional body. On the mental plane you experience it as Light, which surrounds your thoughts. The Ascension column will prepare you for the Ascension waves, when they will happen actually.

## HOW CAN YOU PREPARE?

It is good for you to meditate every day. Meditation makes your contact with the inner being easier; it aligns you with the source of Love inside of yourselves. Listen to yourself how long and when to meditate. You can choose the way of meditation also. You can meditate simply by watching your breath. There are many techniques existing. Know them better. Connect with us. If you have troubles, ask the assistance from the Ascended Masters. And assistance will come. If you doubt, just try. You will be surprised. Be insisting in establishing connections with us. Even if you think there is no response, continue. Sometimes we can not come, because you are not open enough for our presence. Some of you are afraid. There is no reason for fear, but it still appears. Fear exists because of your former experiences in this world. You can release that. We are your friends. We are with you. Love is bringing us together. By deciding for the Ascension you will face the fact that you need to release attachments towards the duality, in which you have lived. You can do that gently and aligned so that you call Archangel Michael in your meditations and ask him to release any connections between you and the third dimensional reality. Then you can open to his loving presence. If you will do that every day your life will be coming better and better. When you will enter into the Light of Ascension waves do not worry about the world that you are leaving behind. Everything will be taken care of. If you have children, they will go with you.

The Ascension means a transition from a zone of the karmic law into a zone of the Divine Grace, which happens through forgiveness. You do not need to pay off your karma, you can release it. So release all resentments that you have for yourself and the others. It would be nice that you would take a piece of paper, write down all your resentments and judgments and release them.

If you like, you can do that once each week. You will see that you will feel much better then. If you feel guilt inside of yourself, which you can not release, talk to a friend who will understand you and will not judge you. Confess to him, tell him about your deeds that you feel were not right. A real connection between two souls will melt the burden of guilt and so you will be relieved. You will discover that you do not need to judge yourself any more, because in your heart, you are the Divine Being. Some of you are quite excited about the news of evacuation. This will happen, but this is only a lifting of your physical bodies. Much more important is a lifting of your consciousness into the Ascended state. The first wave of Ascension can happen any moment, even today. Are you ready, at this moment, to leave your life in duality behind and enter the Light?

A time of great changes is coming. The time is coming when all beings will feel Love in their hearts. So do not be afraid, these are changes to better. A new world is emerging. And you are those, who are creating it. And we are with you.

ASHTAR COMMAND KROTRON STARBASE<br>
IXATAAR INTERCEPT 11:11:83<br>
END OF TRANSMISSION

---

# AWAKENING FROM A DREAM OF DUALITY

Dreams of duality are over. Eternal world of Oneness is beginning...

Greetings, dear brothers and sisters of Light. This is the Ashtar Command, Krotron StarBase. We are with you to represent to you possibilities and ways of preparation, which you can use in your everyday life for your spiritual growth and Ascension process. Because the Ascension is not an event, but a process, which is already taking place. Its culmination are the Ascension waves, lifting upon the ships of the Ashtar Command and lifting of the consciousness in a total Oneness. On this path many techniques and meditations can help you. We shall represent some of them to you but you can decide on your own which you will use. Actually your heart will decide. You will see that meditations can really help you, because when you meditate, we are with you.

## CONNECTION WITH STARRY BROTHERS

You can connect with us anywhere and everywhere. When you feel a need for connection, breath through your heart centre in the middle of your chest and clearly, firmly and peacefully repeat : Ashtar Command. Many of you feel a great connection with Jesus. You can call him. He is also one of us. Your call means that you wish to connect with us and we will send you energy through your heart centre. If you feel that there is no response, insist, because your heart centre needs to be open and ready. And when you call us we will prepare you for this connection. You can breathe and call us while you are at your jobs, doing your work, while walking, driving your car or anything else. You do not need to sit down, close your eyes and meditate to connect. Simply breathe through your heart and think about us.

## RELEASE OF KARMA

You can release your karma with a violet flame. When you feel a blockade in yourself or unpleasant emotional state, you can visualize a violet flame which is coming from the sky, flowing through you and releasing the blockade right to the centre of the Earth, where this blockade is transformed into the Light, into the fire of the Earth. This flame rotates into the anti clockwise direction and is always with you. When you think of it and call it, you increase its effect very much.

If there is a pattern in your life, which is repeating and you can not get rid of it, use the violet flame to carry it away into the fire of Earth. Along with that you can visualize that it carries away from your body all cells which carry the energetic record for this blockade pattern. So the cellular memory for blockade will go away and will make room for Love. If you feel that your heart was wounded in your life, you can visualize a violet flame which carries away all wounds of your heart into the fire of Earth. In order to open your heart you need to heal it first from wounds of the past.

## YOUR ANGELIC PRESENCE

Merge with your inner being, with your Angelic presence. In mediations you can visualize an Angelic being, in a humanlike body. Look into his eyes and feel Love which flows between you. Let the Angel communicate you the Angelic name, this is also your name, because you are one with this Angel. Lift with him among the Stars, flow in the ocean of Cosmic Love and merge into one being. Then you can visualize how you return to Earth, merged with Angel in One.

In everyday life, remember of that as much as possible. Become Angelic being. Feel the Angelic energy inside yourself and spread it around into your neighborhood. Use your Starry name, because this calls for the Angelic presence.

## RELEASING ATTACHMENTS OF DUALITY

In your meditation you can visualize yourself, surrounded by things, people and situations, towards which you are attached. Then you can visualize a mighty Angelic being, which covers all this with its presence. Ask him in your thoughts to set you free of all dependence from the world of duality. Visualize how everything which is not aligned with your highest truth, goes away from your life. And what is aligned in your being stays with you, but you are not attached to that any more. You can visualize this mighty angelic being which ceases all cords of attachment between you and the world of duality. You can experience freedom and release. Thank the Angel for his help. Any time you will feel a need to release from a certain problem or situation, you can call him. He is your ally and friend. Also when you will need protection from energies of the world of duality you can ask him. He will protect you. Any time you call him, he will be with you. We are always with you ...

ASHTAR COMMAND KROTRON STARBASE
IXATAAR INTERCEPT 12:21
END OF TRANSMISSION

---

# LOVE IS THE POWER OF REDEMPTION

The sacredness of beauty of our inner being is that which will redempt us ...

Greetings, our dear Stary brothers and sisters. This is the Ashtar Command, Krotron StarBase in alignment with the mother-ship Excalibur. We are with you and you are with us, to rejoice together the times in which we are and the times which will be coming. Can't you feel awakening of something glorious, like if there is a certain presence in the air, like if there something beautiful will happen. A time of great changes has come, a time when your hearts will be full of joy. Say yes to your heart, which feels the presence of New. Do not listen too much to the doubts of your mind, which does not believe in Ascension and in miracle, which is awakening. Listen to your heart, feel the energy, which is coming. The wind of change began to blow, which will awaken you from the dream of duality, in which you have entangled yourself. You will see signs in the Skies. The comet, which has collided with Jupiter, was such sign. And many more will come. This heralds the rifts in the space-time structure, through which the Divine Love will begin to pure into this world. This is the final time. This is a time of completion. This is a time of redemption which will happen through Love.

## LOVE YOURSELVES

Simply decide. Release your thoughts and go with the flow. Feel Love. Open your heart and trust Love, which is guiding you and nurturing you every moment. Love, which will redempt you. Release a need for feeling guilty, for judging, for being unhappy. This is not needed any more. You have paid off your debts. Redemption will come. It is coming. Regardless of your circumstances, of your troubles, know: time is at hand. Love will come to fill the hearts of thirsty people with water of life. Everything is becoming perfect. What appears imperfect will change into perfect. We are with you, with our etheric technology of liquid Light, to help you. The door of Oneness is open. Energetic vortexes are activated. Ascension on this world can begin. The first wave can happen any moment, when the word from above comes, the instruction of the Cosmic consciousness of One. Everything is ready. You are also ready. You are ready to accept yourselves.

You are ready to live in abundance of spirit and matter. .You are ready to live in harmony. Harmony is inside of you. Find it. Beauty is inside of you. Beauty is guiding you towards Love. Everybody among you is a precious, unique being. You are an indispensable part of the whole. Look how the whole Creation is taking care of you. That what you feel is important for the whole Creation. What you wish is a wish of the whole Creation. Each of you is a part and each of you is a whole. The whole Creation, the whole Cosmos. Each of you is God. Because we are all One. How to love yourself, how to come towards Love? First of all, do not judge yourself. Do not judge the degree of development that you have attained. You are all the Ascended Masters, just you believe otherwise. And your belief manifests itself. You do not need to change your personality to suit some high spiritual ideal. Your personality will fall away anyway. You do not need to be overly concerned about it. You are perfect and O.K. just as you are. Love, truth and beauty inside of you are perfect. Be gentle with yourself. Do not force yourself too much. Take your time to rest. Enjoy the beauty. Love every of your thoughts, every of your feelings, even if they are not yet harmonious. Love your anger, your fear, your doubts. Love your body. Body goes with you along into the Ascension. Love your sexual energy that will go along with you into the Ascension, along with your body. Love everything that you are. Give yourself everything that you need. Fill yourself with gifts, attention, abundance. And when you will be full to brink, share this with others. Connect with them.

Talk to each other. Touch each other. Kiss each other. Merge with each other. Share love with each other, drink love from the depth of Oneness.

Be, what you are. Believe in that what you feel. Be that what you feel, be true, be whole. Resolve all unfinished in your life. Release all untrue. You don't have any time for compromises. Act according to that. And invite us to be with you. To merge with you. And our Love is your Love and our consciousness will merge with yours into One: in a consciousness of Ascended Masters - Heaven and Earth.

ASHTAR COMMAND KROTRON STARBASE
IXATAAR INTERCEPT 12:21
END OF TRANSMISSION

---

# LAW OF MANIFESTATION

Hard thoughts of duality have created frozen world. Soft, liquid thoughts of Oneness will melt it ...

Hello, dear friends. This is the Ashtar Command, Krotron StarBase. We are with you and you are with us to rejoice together the times in which we are, the times of Ascension, the times when a door of Oneness is open. You've opened it with your belief, with your decision, because you believe. And it's always like that. You create your reality with your decisions. As you decide, so it is. Always. This world, in which you live, was not created by anybody outside of yourselves. You have created it by yourself, with your beliefs, which densified the energy of liquid Light to that extent that it appears as solid matter. So we could say that the world that you are into, Is your frozen thought. And because once you have thought the duality thoughts, you have found yourself in a frozen world of duality. You have believed that you are sinners and it occurred along with your belief. And you called this karma.

In a world like that you have lived many lifetimes. But slowly, a wish to return to Oneness has awakened in your hearts. And this wish activated the decision, which caused a changing of the world in which you live. Because once that you accept decision, which is aligned with your inner being, the whole Creation helps you to carry it out. But you need to do the first step and attain clarity about what you want and what you would like in your heart. And then you act in accordance with that, and express this with your deeds and words.

## THE IMPORTANCE OF YOUR DECISION

Your decision is very important. With your decision you trigger a cycle of manifestation, with your decision everything begins to happen. The energy begins to gather and if you are insistent enough and firm at your decision, if you water your vision with soft attention, it will soon yield results. This works regardless of what you want. If you wish to have abundance, make a decision and you will have it. If you would like to have happiness, make your decision, and you'll have it. Because liquid Light in your world is densified in quite dense matter, you'll wait sometimes for the results of your decision. You can accelerate the manifestation process if you connect with us. If you call us in your thoughts and with few words shortly, clearly and accurately say to us what you want, that will do. We will hear you and help to manifest your wishes if they are aligned with your inner being. And most of your wishes are. So do not hesitate and turn to us for help. Insist in doing that and the results will be seen soon. With our etheric technology we can accelerate a process of manifestation in your world to some extent and make it easier. We would like to make your life as easy as possible, because you are our beloved ones. And when you receive a gift from us, receive it with thankfulness, because thankfulness opens your hearts to receive more.

## BEAUTY IS GUIDING YOU IN A NEW WORLD

Ascension waves which are ahead of you are a consequence of your common decision to return into the world of Oneness. Dimensional opening of the 11 : 11 enables your transition in the new reality which you have decided for. So transfer your attention from the old reality, which you are leaving behind, into the new one, which you are entering. Because energy is flowing in the direction which your attention dictates. If you orientate towards the new world, if you create it in your everyday life, it will soon appear for the whole humanity. The critical mass for the quantum leap of the consciousness of humanity will be reached in a few years. In the new world your thoughts will be manifested instantaneously, because the matter will become much more fluid and will respond on the energies of spirit more quickly. Actually Spirit and Matter will become One. Miracles will happen, which are the natural expression of Love in Cosmos. It is important for you now that you live in accordance with your highest truth for this transition in the new reality.

So release your compromises and imperfections from your life. Compromises are not your highest good, not even the highest good of the whole. In your reality they exist until you decide differently. You can change the reality, which you created with your thoughts, so that it aligns with your highest good. And the highest good is the Divine Plan, where everything is perfect, where everybody has his place and purpose.

See the Light of the truth in your heart and follow it. Through beauty it will show you the way. Go, where the beauty is. Do not occupy yourself with that which does not evoke a feeling of beauty. Do not enlarge that with your attention. Follow beauty, wherever you see it. So there will be more of it in your life, and when the transition point will be reached, beauty will overflow this world and change it into the point of Light.

When doubts and fears appear do not yield yourself to them. That what is true will remain. When you will be ready to release your fears and doubts, the Cosmic Divine Plan will be revealed to you in all its beauty. You will discover that Cosmic Love is taking care of you every moment, and that you live in abundance of spirit and matter, that you are acting outwards as a soul, as Angelic Starry Being. You can get rid of your fears and doubts by writing down the positive and the negative affirmations, for example: I am rich, I am poor. By doing that something will happen in your consciousness, you will set yourself free from being caught in any mental state and then you could decide freely, whether you wish to be wealthy or poor. And it will happen, as you believe. You can do that once a week, with those mental states which you feel most captured in. It is good in these times not to be overly attached to anybody or anything. Because many things and people will go away from your life, because they are not in a resonance with your highest truth any more. They will go to make room for new, more beautiful, more true. So do not be afraid of changes that are coming. Do not resist them. Those changes are guiding you into a new, miraculous world.

And we go with you ...

ASHTAR COMMAND KROTRON STARBASE
IXATAAR INTERCEPT 12:21
END OF TRANSMISSION

---

# ATLANTIS I

Pleiades were once the Atlantis and are connected with the Atlantis and its seven races .

The history of Atlantis and even earlier civilizations was not known for a long time. Let us look at this past from a perspective of STAR PEOPLE. Most of STAR PEOPLE who are now on Earth, began their evolutionary path, by entering Angelic form of life from Oneness through the Central Sun in this or neighbor Galaxy M 31 in Andromeda, which is a twin soul to our Galaxy. And the host of Starry Angelic Beings have split throughout the Galaxy and transferred from one Galaxy to the other. And most all STAR PEOPLE who are now on the Earth, have achieved a degree of Archangel (which in human evolution equals to a grade of Ascended Master) inside the Local logos. Local logos is a Star field in this Galaxy, which is so wide that Light needs thousand years to travel across it.

Inside the Local logos the Star Beings have gathered around certain stars, which serve as a Star gate into higher dimensions.

There we have developed our Archangel consciousness. Among the Star gates the most important is the Orion constellation, which acts as an Antarion conversion. In the upper part of Orion there is a star called Betelgeuse - which is a home of the White Magicians, and in the lower part of Orion there is a star called Rigel, where Black magicians have lived.

The central part of Orion is an area of alchemistic fusion of Darkness and Light, so it can become a dimensional window from the Local logos evolution into the Galactic evolution of Oneness. This dimensional window is created by three stars in the belt of Orion, called EL AN RA, which hold the whole area of Local logos into position. The central star of those three represents the transition zone into the unmanifested cosmic levels. Planet Earth is connected with the constellation of Orion, because in the Atlantean times it was under strong influence of the Dark Lords and represents a zone for the experiment of duality.

Pleiades are also an important Star gate. The brightest star in Pleiades, Alcyone, is the Central Sun of the Local logos. Around that star an etheric planet of beautiful green color orbited once, called Ajaho in Pleiadian starry language. Many Star beings have lived there as Ascended Angels in perfect Oneness. We were achieving experiences about the vibration of matter and of merger of consciousness - Cosmic Tantra. This is the first Atlantis, which is the source of a later Atlantean civilization on Earth. 18 million years ago the Pleiades have densified from etheric towards physical plane and at that time the planet Ajaho exploded.

Sirius is a star gate, one of the closest to our Solar System. Around Sirius an etheric planet of a beautiful blue color orbited, and on that planet Star beings lived in etheric bodies. They were similar to earthly dolphins. Some of them are incarnated as people or as dolphins on planet Earth.

Now, on Sirius, there is a brotherhood called Og-min, the Blue Lodge of Sirius, which takes care of the development of the Galactic network of Light in this sector of the Galaxy. Aside Sirius there are many more star gates in the Local logos such as Antares, Aldebaran, Arcturus, Big Dipper including the North Polar Star.

Local Logos was chosen for an experiment of duality, which will, by its completion, enable the healing of Darkness of the whole Galaxy, and with that the fulfillment of the very old prophecy about the creation of the Galactic network of Light. In this experiment some Starry beings have taken the role of

Light, other Star beings role of Black Magicians and they began to fight with each other and judge themselves. And now this experiment is completing. It completes by everybody forgiving themselves and others and by choosing Love as a power of redemption by their free will. Experiences in the world of duality enable us to set us free from the boundaries of the Local Logos and to enter the Galactic evolution of Oneness. The wisdom, which we have achieved in the world of duality, enables us to understand Darkness. It allows us to transform and heal with Love the Darkness of the whole Galaxy.

## LEMURIA

On Earth an experiment started 7 million years ago, when time has come for human race to reach individuation. Individuation is a process during which the living being begins to become conscious about himself, it is a transition from the animal to the Human Kingdom. At that time many Starry beings came to assist Earth. A host of Starry Beings was gathered by Lords of Fire, very evolved beings, who were guided by Sanat Kumara. Lords of Fire had two missions. They have activated the Star codes of 11:11 in the Light bodies of the STAR PEOPLE, and those codes activate at a suitable moment and guarantee that no Starry being can lose himself completely in the world of duality. And the second mission was to create bodies of Light for Human beings: Around every Divine spark two bodies of Light were created, so called twin souls. Thus Man was created.

After that all Lords of Fire, except seven, went away. Seven of them gathered Starry volunteers and together they have landed on the White Island in Mongolia and created a City of Light there, where they lived. In later times when the circumstances on Earth were worsened, the City of Light removed itself to an etheric plane and received a name Shamballa.

Other part of the Starry family remained in Space and gathered around Earth in etheric Cities of Light, which we could call Star ships today. At that time Galactic Confederation was established and the Ashtar Command also. Starry Beings who remained upon the ships assisted in building a planetary and Interstellar network of Light.

This was a period of Lemuria. In those times of the third race people were Giants, as much as 10 meters high, with their third eye developed and with an ability to materialize, but spiritually they were hardly any more developed as animals were. In the earlier periods of Lemuria people were hermaphrodites, but slowly they began to separate on men and women. The Starry beings that have landed on Earth helped Lemurians with their development. By the end of Lemuria, a primitive speech developed, first forms of the primitive art appeared also. A cult of physical body appeared and people have raised huge statues of physical bodies in natural size. You can still see such statues on the Easter Islands, where there once was a city of Lemuria. In a latter period of Lemuria people began to mate with animals, which caused genetic degeneration.. Three to four million years ago Lemuria sank down into the Pacific Ocean in a serial of volcanic eruptions. Space ships of the Ashtar Command rescued many people and moved them into Australia and South America, especially around Lake Titicaca.

# ATLANTIS II

In those days there was a Land of the west called Aztlan. Many generations ago, priests of White Star came from there and they have brought wisdom to our planet...

Before Lemuria went down Manu gathered the best representatives of Lemurian race and with genetic engineering created Atlanteans. First Atlanteans populated huge islands in the middle of Atlantic Ocean. The first Atlantean race was black skinned and was called Rmoahall. Rmoahalls fought with the remnants of Lemurians for space. Soon, the second Atlantean race developed, which was called Tlavatli. Tlavatlis worshipped the Sun, they were shamen.

The true rise of Atlantis began one million years ago, when the Toltec race developed. Toltec (which are not the same as the Indian tribe Toltek) created a beautiful civilization, full of abundance and wealth, which was called Tollan Tlapallan. In the City of Golden Gate rich buildings were erected, which were made of red, white and black stone, full of gold and precious stones. A Mystery School was created, where the most advanced Atlanteans could go on spiritual path in the Triple Temple. Starry People have guided the Atlantis wisely as Kings and Priests under careful guidance of the Galactic Confederation. This was the Golden Era of Atlantis, which lasted more than hundred thousand years.

Prosperity of Atlantis was interrupted by coming of the Dark Lords from Orion. Orions began to program STAR PEOPLE with electronic equipment. This process is called implantation. STAR PEOPLE have received their first implants voluntarily in order that they could carry out their role in experiment of duality. In that way we have left our Ascended state of a Master of Wisdom and lowered our vibration, we began to forget who we are, and began to merge with human race. We began to incarnate alternatively between Black and White Magicians to know Good and Evil.

In Mystery School a split manifested, the City of Golden Gate and Toltec Civilization declined, and long magical wars on Heaven and Earth began. Galactic Confederation announced Earth as a quarantine area. Dark Lords from Orion resisted the instructions from Confederation, so therefore many of them were expelled or destroyed.

In a huge natural cataclysm 869.000 years ago the first deluge of Atlantis happened. After the deluge southern areas of Atlantis were swampy and not suitable for populating. On other areas Kingdom of Aztlan came into the existence. The Great Mystery School with the dynasty of Divine Kings, Ascended Masters, gradually moved into Egypt. The residues of the Dark Lords continued with the magical wars. Genetic blending between STAR PEOPLE and Earthlings began. 212.000 years ago the second deluge happened which split Atlantis in two big islands.

After the second deluge strengthening came from Pleiades, which established civilization again. On northern island Toltec race rose again which built a beautiful city of Colardan, and in the area of current Ireland, the Kingdom of Danaan flowered. Science about colors sounds and smells expanded. Crystals were wide spread and were used for healing, implantation, as energetic generators, as data banks and as light resources. Atlanteans mastered the materialization with strong magnetic fields and they have built their cities with this technology. Under the water many dome cities were made, which were connected with huge system of underneath tunnels. For a long distance transport the higher castes representatives used teleportation chambers. At that time people were selected in seven castes, based upon the degree of spiritual development. Higher castes of Priests, which were made of STAR PEOPLE, developed their mental body, especially the ability of telepathy, and were subjected to intense occult training. Lower castes developed their emotional body. The membrane between the physical and astral plane was much thinner in Atlantis and therefore the astral world much more interweaved with the physical one. The priests became obsessed with power and began to manipulate the masses with magic, genetic engineering and implantation. They were maintaining control by implanting mental patterns of separation between Man and God and separation between Love and Sexuality. The centre of control was the Oralin temple, in the middle of Colardan city, where the Ashtar crystal stood. There from the control of all life in Atlantis took place. The new deluge was coming and the priests had foreseen that. They have built 3 pyramids in Egypt and those pyramids contained all knowledge of Atlantis. The Masters guided the withdrawal of people towards Asia, where Manu created the new race at the Kailas Mountain, and this race is a base of current civilization. The Divine Kings, Ascended Masters have withdrawn along with some conscious STAR PEOPLE back to the ships of the Ashtar Command. Some of them have returned to Pleiades, where they still have a very beautifully developed civilization. Because of misuse the Ashtar crystal exploded and caused a deluge 75.025 years B.C.

After the third deluge there was only a small island remaining from Atlantis, and this island is called Poseidonis now. Strengthening came from Sirius, which tried to establish civilization again, but Atlantis was decaying more and more. Masters of Wisdom were not present on Earth any more. The Atlantis was ruled by Kings who were already implanted, so their wisdom was not perfect any more. The experiment of duality went closer and closer to its end. One stellar cycle ago, that is 25.800 years ago, a wave of Star Children came to Earth and those Star Children have in their genetic material the codes for transition from Duality into Oneness. 16.000 years ago the Jupiter Command received instructions for establishing the Order of the Star on Earth from the Blue Lodge of Sirius. Its mission is to choose Love with freewill as a power of redemption and therefore to complete the experiment of duality. Representatives of the Order of the Star have been discovering the techniques of healing and removing of implants. They have built a Sphinx near the pyramids in Egypt, and disciples of the Mystery School could receive their first spiritual initiation there. Below the Sphinx there was a crystal data bank with all knowledge of Atlantis. But for Atlantis it was already too late. At the year 9.564 B.C. it sank completely. After the deluge the dynasty of Divine Kings tried to reestablish the Atlantis again in Egypt but it was just a glorious decay. Atlantean wisdom and knowledge were sinking into forgetfulness more and more.

Ample floods in a year 3.111 B.C. destroyed those last remnants. 5.000 years long period of Darkness began and the Atlantis was forgotten and with the Atlantis also the purpose of the experiment of duality.

This experiment is now completing itself. In the second decade of this century Krishnamurti renewed the Order of the Star on the physical plane. On inner planes many representatives of the Order of the Star were working and bringing to humanity the techniques and methods of healing. The split is healing, the separation is merging back into Oneness. Many STAR PEOPLE are awakening, many are deciding for transition into the world of Oneness. And so slowly, a New Atlantis is emerging, a world of Ascended Masters on Earth ...

# CONVERSION VORTICES

This is the Ashtar Command, Krotron StarBase. We are with you and you are with us to birth together the New Reality. Currently we are all in a stage of transition inside the doorway of the 11:11. This transition brings forth new forms of love and relating. Until the third gate activation a vast transformation was taking place, which will build the foundation of the New Reality. Until the third gate activation a network of conversion vortices was be established and they will be the core of internal and external islands of Light in the Octave Seven on the New Earth.

Conversion vortices are double spiral conversion / inversion stations which turn duality into Oneness, visible into Invisible. They are starry mandalas of Ascension, inner islands of Light which externalize themselves. They are creating an energy field of Ascending beauty which transcends into Miraculous. These vortices anchor the dimensional axis of 11:11:83. Because of the sacredness of their beauty, they are surrounded by the dimensional sphere of divine grace, emanating from the Galactic Central Sun System.

These vortices are created by individuals, coming together as One. Old perception of duality, which allows only two beings to be intimately together, is greatly expanded. Many beings form a group, unite and merge in sacred intimate Oneness and thus create a starry Mandala. Their fluid relationships allow the Mandala to repattern itself and spiral higher into even greater Oneness. Anchored deeply into One Heart, their physical closeness and sexual openness towards each other allows the Heavenly Love and the Earthly Love of duality to come together, Ascend and thus form a dimensional sphere of True Love, emanating from Oneness.

Each one of you is creating his own conversion vortex. It is the process of birthing the Invisible into visible through magnetic manifestation, bringing scattered fragments of our starry essence together into the dimensional axis of 11:11:83. Your conversion vortices on Earth are coming together, merging, repatterning and restructuring themselves, connecting with our conversion vortices in the sky and creating together a pulsating network of Liquid Light around this planet that forms the Antarion Conversion.

Each of conversion vortices emerges from a True Love relationship, which is symbolized by a point in the centre of the Mandala. True Love is another being which connects with you in a love relationship. This may be your twin soul or your soul mate which is overshadowed by your twin soul, this latter in a case when your twin soul is not incarnated or not in a suitable position to form a love relationship with you. This True Love relationship creates a double pillar of Miraculous, which forms the core of the dimensional axis 11:11:83, leading to the Galactic Central Sun System and then Beyond the Beyond, into the One.

This is surrounded with many soul mate relationships, which are activated by the law of magnetic attraction. They serve as transformation points in the energy field of Liquid Light. They are symbolized by a six pointed star.

This is surrounded further with more soul family relationships, which create the energy field of Liquid Light. This is the foundation of the Template of True Love. It is symbolized by a circle which encircles the six pointed star.

All these different interlocking levels of union create wheels within wheels of spiral movements which form the Ascending flame into Octave Seven. In Octave Eleven, this Mandala is restructured. Fusion of Heaven and Earth is achieved and transcended, so physical matter Ascends and ceases to be. Thus the starry Mandala is turned inside out and expanded. It forms the fabric of the New Reality, expanding into Invisible beyond the realms of the New Earth, leading ever deeper into One.

ASHTAR COMMAND KROTRON STARBASE
IXATAAR INTERCEPT 11:11:83
END OF TRANSMISSION

---

# GALACTIC TANTRA

... because your dream in this world is clear and eternal ...

Hello, our dear Starry brothers and sisters. This is the Ashtar Command, Krotron StarBase. We are with you and you are with us to look together at the process of merger, which begins to take place between you. Your world is traveling through the ring of Light and is exposed towards increased presence of the energies of the Galactic Central Sun, which enable the development of cosmic consciousness through relationships among you, especially between a man and a woman. The whole Universe, in which you exist, is maintained by equilibrium of male and female energies.

The merger of male and female energies in this Cosmos causes the transition from Duality into Oneness. And what is occurring in the Cosmic scale, is occurring also among you. This process of merger is called the Galactic Tantra.

This is a process, during which you meet each other. You meet as men and women and as Angelic Beings simultaneously. The Oneness among you is established by changing energies on all levels of existence. Real connection is made by surrendering to each other, by surrendering to the beauty that you see in each other. This beauty represents a doorway into Oneness. In order to feel that you need to allow yourself to be close to each other, to listen to your heart, and not to your fears.

Along with the openness, a tendency for getting closer and merger is needed also. A tendency for getting closer is that focused energy, which causes merger. It is the Divine will in your heart. Once a contact is established you strengthen it with sincere communication, with empathy and physical contact. The contact so deepens and when all the energies that you feel are expressed, it transforms into a pure Cosmic Love, it transcends a relationship between a man and a woman. Two beings or a group of beings merge into one Cosmic Angelic Being of Light. During the transition through the opening the 11:11 into the world of Oneness, you will meet beings, soul mates, and you will connect with them in intimate relationships. In those relationships you will find fulfillment. Therefore it is important to release all relationships that do not bring you happiness in your life. Of course, you can only do that when you forgive all people with love.

Your will meet your ideal mate. It is the Divine Plan for everybody, who decides for a transition into the world of Oneness. It is good for you to be prepared for that, because the relationship that you have towards each other can be only as good as a relationship that you have to yourself. So therefore you will not meet your other half until you will learn to accept yourself and until you will not be living in the world of Oneness with your consciousness. And when this meeting will happen it will be a great change for the better. You will experience intimate Oneness and a merge of two beings in infinity. You will feel Cosmic Love, which will bring harmonic alignment between you, All compromises will fall away. Duality is not an acceptable reality any more.

You will connect in groups with other STAR PEOPLE. In those groups a healing of interpersonal relationships will take place. Intimacy will rule among everybody in the group. Jealousy and possessiveness will fall away. Trust will develop. Taboos of the world of duality regarding touching and exchange of sexual energy will be transcended. Certain parts of the body exist in the world of duality that people usually do not touch. This conditions your consciousness and it is wonderful to transcend this conditioning. Also you suppress a flow of sexual energy many times. You do not need to express it in a sexual intercourse. Sometimes it is enough to express it through a gentle touch. It is enough to feel it, to let it live and it will transform into Love. In groups of Oneness you will develop a support towards each other, you will be allies. These groups will become Ascension Stars in the Planetary network of Light.

Meet each other, create groups, touch each other, merge together. Merge together, release all guilt, be happy. Because your joy is our joy. We are with you

ASHTAR COMMAND KORTRON STARBASE
ISIS INTERSECTION 11:11:83/12:21
END OF TRANSMISSION

# ISLANDS OF LIGHT

Oases of new reality are emerging, zones of no-time in a chaos of the final days ...

Hello, our dear brothers and sisters. This is the Ashtar Command, Krotron StarBase. We are with you and you are with us to create together Heaven on Earth. Merger of Heaven and Earth will begin to happen in the zones of new reality, in Islands of Light. These are communities of New Age, where people will decide consciously for the transition into the world of Oneness and with their decision they will allow new reality to come among them. You are namely creating your reality with your decisions and with your mutual agreements. And if you agree for a transition into the world of Oneness, it actually happens. Your Planet is transiting from the zone of Duality in a zone of Oneness and you can decide to go in Oneness along with it. Islands of Light began to be established from the 12th of December 1994, when Earth entered through the 12:12 Star Gate and was set free of the densest energies of duality. This was the day, when the New Age began to manifest in physical world. This was the day, when this world began to enter deeper levels of dimensional opening the 11:11 more freely.

Soul families, soul mates and twin souls will be gathering in the Islands of Light. New interpersonal relationships will be established among them, which will transcend separation between sexual and Love energy, and separation between Man and God. Intimate connections will be created in those groups on all levels of existence, including physical. So a merge of Heaven and Earth will be created. Those open intimate connections will represent a magnet for energies of Cosmic Love and Divine Grace. They will anchor Oneness in your physical world. Energetic vortexes will be created, which will lift the consciousness of the whole group from Duality into Oneness. In such groups, a process of Ascension, a process of a group initiation in a world of Oneness will take place.

In Islands of Light you will develop intensive cooperation among yourselves and especially intensive cooperation with us. Representatives of the Ashtar Command live in splendid Islands of Light in the Sky, which you call Space ships. We could live in open Space but for many reasons we decide to settle in luminous cities, ships, Starry Islands of Light. We believe namely in beauty and that's why we surround ourselves with beauty, wherever we go. Between your and our Islands of Light energetic flow will be established through time. Every Island of Light that you will create, will accept from us an Etheric StarBase, which will float highly above it and surround it with energetic pillar of Ascension.

In every Island of Light at least one Ascended Master will be present in his physical body. Though the first Islands of Light will be established very soon they will expand much more after the volunteers of the first wave of Ascension will come back to the Earth as Ascended Masters. Many of them will establish Islands of Light.

Islands of Light will be created in areas that are extremely clear energetically. They will be created in purity of thoughts, feelings and deeds. But before all, in a total surrender to the world of Oneness, because all communities which are based on the world of duality will fall apart in the following years. It is very important for the Islands of Light to be totally self-reliant. Self-reliant, which regards energetic sources, which regards food and financial means. In great changes that will reach your world, Islands of Light will be islands of peace and stability in the midst of chaos. STAR PEOPLE will come from there into the world and help it in its transition into the new dimension. The Islands of Light will be the only points, which will remain untouched, because they will be existing in a consciousness of the higher dimension even before. So therefore it is important to create Islands of Light in a totally clear consciousness.

## HOW TO CREATE ISLANDS OF LIGHT?

The first phase of creating Islands of Light is happening inside of yourselves. The process of growth is a process of preparation for a common living in the Islands of Light. Therefore it is beautiful to learn from interpersonal relationships and to work upon yourself. It is good you express your Angelic presence that you feel inside. And you say: " I forgive myself for I am not of this world. Islands of Light that we will create are not of this world. But they will be in this world to lift it in a point of Light."

You are meeting your Starry families and gathering in different groups. All this is a preparation for living in Islands of Light. Many of you feel internal yearning for living in Islands of Light. Some of you have already tried to create communities inside the groups that you are belonging to.

The second phase of establishing the Islands of Light begins when all those who feel this yearning for Islands of Light gather together regardless of what group they are belonging to. Actually it is not needed for them to belong to any group. In your country, many projects of communal living appeared and when they will merge together, such community will finally begin to manifest in a physical world as well.

All New Age groups in California are namely a part of the same vortex, which has its centre in Los Angeles and is one of the twelve major energetic vortexes of New Age on Earth. Therefore the Island of Light in your country will be established near Los Angeles. And Los Angeles will be white city, a city of Light. And your country will be a green country, a country of Love. And your world will be a blue Planet, a point of

Light in the Galactic network of Light. And we will become all One

ASHTAR COMMAND KROTRON STARBASE
IXATAAR INTERCEPT 12:21
END OF TRANSMISSION

---

# STARRY STONES

... and Starry stones fell from the Sky, to guard us that we do not forget that we are sons and daughters of the Stars ...

Hello, our dear Angels. This is the Ashtar Command, Krotron StarBase. We are with you and you are with us that we tell you that you are not alone on this world as Starry beings. When you came to this world from the Cosmic depths, Starry stones came with you and they help you in these times to remember where did you come from and where are you going. Those stones are interdimensional doorways in higher dimensions of the world of Oneness. There are many dimensions in this Cosmos. You know the three-dimensional world very well. This is a world of duality in which you have lived many lifetimes on Earth in absence of Love. Actually a world like that is an extreme rarity in this Cosmos. Most worlds in this Cosmos are worlds of Oneness, worlds of Universal Light. Cosmic Love is a basic force which creates this Universe and many miracles in it. It is full of beautiful Starry nebulae, rainbow planets. Black and white holes, spiral galaxies, dimensional Star gates and openings, when amazing whirlpools of space and time in undreamed of dimensions are happening. There are the worlds of the fifth dimension and even higher dimensions which you will enter finally upon your Ascension. But in those dimensions you can begin to enter right now. Starry stones that are here with you on Earth enable you to do that.

## USE OF STARRY STONES

Starry stones that we speak to you about came to you from Star gates in the area of Local Logos. In your language these stones are called tektites. Different sorts of tektites exist which come from various Stars of the Local Logos and they can connect you with the interdimensional energies of those stars. Tektites are the stones of Oneness, Masters of mineral Kingdom. They are pure liquid Light. No thought of duality can enter their interior, so you do not need to cleanse them. You can not program those stones. They act on their own by their beautiful presence. You can wear them in your jewelery or use them in your meditations, by holding them in your hands. They act most beautifully in their natural shape, uncut. They go along well with meteorites, amethysts and quartz crystals. Very clear quartz crystals which are called Herkimer diamonds are extremely suitable for this connection. They are invoking the energies of Ascension, energies of divine intervention, which raise your consciousness towards the consciousness of Ascended Masters. You can arrange those stones in a shape of various symbols and create a Mandala, which will accelerate your Ascension path. Especially effective is a Mandala in a form of six-pointed Star.

## VARIETIES OF STARRY STONES

Among Starry stones the most known is Moldavite. This stone has a beautiful green color. It comes from Pleiades. When 18 million years ago the planet Ajaho, which orbited around Alcyone exploded, one part of this planet fell on Earth in the area of current Bohemia, after several million years of journey. In time of Atlantis Moldavite was a stone of the Holy Grail. The purpose of Moldavite is to awaken STAR PEOPLE. Each piece of Moldavite has its own message, which activates your star codes. If you feel alienation from the third dimensional word, it can help you at awakening towards your Starry Home. It can heal your wounded heart and connect you with us. It can help you to anchor your Angelic Starry presence in your physical body. It guides and directs you towards your soul mates and twin souls. Moldavite is the most important stone in a transition to the world of Oneness.

The second form of tektite, which is also quite wide spread, comes from Indonesia and China. You call them tektites or Indokinites. They have black color. Their source is in Star Gate AN in Orion. This is the Star of Galactic Oneness and your astronomers call it Al Nilam. Those stones came to Earth at the beginning of the experiment of duality, 870.000 years ago. They hold a key for a completion of duality and its transcendence. Indokinites have a power to raise the vibration of their surroundings from Duality into Oneness.

Tektites of beautiful violet-brown color came from Sirius. They are called Saffordites. They fell only on one spot in Arizona, therefore they are quite rare. Similar to them are Columbianites, that were found in Colombia in South America and they also came from Sirius. Both have an extremely high vibration so therefore they are suitable only for awakened STAR PEOPLE, who know already their Divine mission and carry it out. Certain pieces of Saffordites have found their way towards STAR PEOPLE all over the world, who were taking part in 12:12 door activation. At that time this stone was activated and began to carry out its true function. It will assist in removing implants from time of Atlantis. It will melt all boundaries in lives of STAR PEOPLE and expand your consciousness into a consciousness of Cosmic Love and Divine Grace.

Many more forms of tektites exist. Libyan tektites which come from Rigel, Bediasites which come from the Horsehead nebula, Georgia tektites, Tibetan tektites (which were once called Agni mani - fire stone, because they cause the raise of kundalini), Irgihzites and many others. Their purpose will be revealed at the right time.

Starry stones are your friends. Connect with them to bring you in the world of the Cosmic beauty. And through them connect with us....

ASHTAR COMMAND KROTRON
STARBASE
IS:IS INTERSECTION 11:11:83/12:21
END OF TRANSMISSION

# LIFE IN PLEIADES

Two Suns are shining on Ajaho. One of them is big and blue and other one is small and orange. There is our home, far away from here.

Hello, Light Beings. This is the Ashtar Command, Krotron StarBase. We are with you and you are with us to look together the life of our Star brothers and sisters from Pleiades. Pleiades were once a source of Angelic beings, which came later on your world as Angelic Ascended beings of Light and helped to create the civilization of Atlantis. When third deluge of Atlantis happened 77.000 years ago as a result of misuse of technology, part of Starry beings decided to come back to Pleiades and try to live in a more harmonic way. Other part of Starry beings decided to remain on Earth and to continue to help earthlings. Many of you belong to that part. Many of you have gone through the Angelic evolution in the Starry system of Pleiades in the distant past.

Starry beings that escaped from Atlantis are still living in Pleiades now. They have been using Atlantean technology for positive purposes and so they slowly created Eden like existence. They have reached harmony of mind and emotions. Their civilization populates more than one hundred planets, which are spread throughout the Pleiades. The main planet is orbiting around the central Sun Alcyone. This planet is full of beautiful vegetation of green color, which is also the color of the sky. Pleiadians have mastered their physical environment and they are regulating weather, which is always nice. They live in crystal cities of Light of beautiful shapes, among vegetation and liquid water, which pours out of the fountains. They believe in beauty so therefore they incarnate in beautiful physical bodies. Their shape is very similar to human although their body is much more beautiful and much more refined. Pleiadians live in communities, in soul families, sometimes they choose also their life partner. They are open towards each other, love flows freely among them. These are joyous beings, full of harmony and happiness. They like to laugh, but not on account of other. Support and understanding rule among them. Many among them are artists, they like music, they like to create.

## LIQUID LIGHT

Etheric technology of liquid Light is very important in life of Pleiadians. Liquid Light is densified etheric substance, which beings of Light can shape with their thoughts. For this purpose pure thoughts and feelings are needed. Liquid Light is used very much by artists in Pleiades who create multidimensional sculptures from it. These are enlivened clouds of rainbow colors Light which float in the air. If anybody touches them or directs his thoughts into them, they align with his vibration. They align their shape and color to this vibration, but they can also emit harmonic sounds or beautiful fragrances. All this affects consciousness of individual and aligns it with Cosmic beauty. A life art of liquid Light is the most important form of expression in Pleiades, especially for musicians and sculptors, who unite both in multidimensional whole. Liquid Light adorns and fills the interior of most of dwellings in Pleiades.

They use etheric technology of liquid Light for materialization of physical objects which they need. Light ships which Pleiadians need for interdimensional interstellar travels are made of densified liquid Light. Those ships are traveling through dimensional Star gates by the use of mental projection. The speed that they can attain in this way is million times greater than the speed of light. Travel from Pleiades to your planet lasts only a couple of hours. Liquid Light in Pleiades has replaced physical technology almost completely. Last physical machines and Star ships were made a couple of thousand years ago, but they still function. Physical technology in Pleiades attained perfection at that time and machines can work many hundreds thousand years without breaking down.

## ASCENSION IN PLEIADES

The time is coming when Pleiadians will master their physical world and the whole Pleiadian civilization will ascend. The ring of Light reached Pleiades in the year of 2002 of your linear time. After that time there will be the Ascension wave in Pleiades. Three waves like on Earth are not needed there, as Pleiadians are much more ready for Ascension. Pleiadian Star ships cooperate with the Ashtar Command for quite some time and they help also with transformation of the Earth into the point of Light.

When the ring of Light reaches Pleiades, this Star system will be ascended through the dimensional doorway the 11:11 in the zone of the Octave eleven and so it will enter the Galactic evolution of Oneness. Some Ascended beings from Pleiades will travel onward to Orion. There they will go through the dimensional doorway AND into higher dimensions of the spiral of Oneness beyond the unknown. And some of us and some of you will join them as well...

ASHTAR COMMAND KROTRON
STARBASE
IXATAAR INTERCEPT 11:11:83
END OF TRANSMISSION

# ENTERING THE NEW AGE

On the 12th of December 1994 Earth begun its entry into the Golden Age. 144.000 beings of Light co created the miracle of redemption...

Hello dear Beings of Light. This is the Ashtar command, Krotron StarBase. We are with you and you are with us to speak about the dimensional doorway 12:12. This dimensional doorway heralded the beginning of manifestation of a New age in your physical world. For this activation 1.000 to 2.000 beings were needed at the pyramids in Egypt and 144.000 around the world. On that day energy of redemption came from Star Sirius through the great pyramid in Egypt towards Earth. This energy set you free from the law of karma, which was ruling in the world of duality. Instead of law of Karma, the law of Divine Grace was established. Divine Grace happens through forgiveness, through Divine intervention, because in your essence you are all Divine and you deserve Love, you are worthy for Ascension. So therefore 12:12 was an extreme opportunity to decide for your transition into the higher state of consciousness, for your ultimate liberation.

Make your decision, believe and it will happen after your belief in the next years. Dimensional doorway of 12:12 meant a great leap of consciousness, which triggers the energies of completion. Those energies enabled you to complete your Divine missions on Earth. That means that you will be free from all limitations, that you will enter a real freedom.

In preparations of the 12:12 activation your Planet needed to be released from the densest energies of duality. Therefore in the autumn months before the 12th of December very intense emotional cleansing was taking place for many of you. This time was an opportunity for you for extreme growth, for cleansing of lower energetic centers. When lower chakras are purified, your emotional body becomes a clear transmitter of Cosmic Love.

## WHAT HAPPENED AFTER 12:12

12:12 is the last planetary activation, which happened in evolutionary sphere of Local Central Sun, inside the spiral of duality. From there on all planetary activations are taking place in the spiral of Oneness inside the dimensional opening of the 11:11. Compared with the magnificence of the opening of 11:11, a 12:12 is just a drop in the Ocean. Despite that the energies of 12:12 accelerated your growth very much. For some of you this was a beginning of quantum leaps of consciousness into higher dimensions. Your development will not be linear any more, but it will become multidimensional. Soon after the 12:12 three outer planets changed their astrological sign and this caused great changes in your world. Waterfalls of Light began to pour on Earth. This is creating conditions for the first wave of Ascension; Ascended Masters will begin to walk among the people. Activity of extraterrestrial civilizations will increase very much. More and more people will be reporting on contacts with extraterrestrial beings. Because of the greater energetic alignments more and more of you will be meeting your soul mates and twin souls. Your perception of time will begin to change dramatically. Zones of no-time will begin to appear, and Miraculuos will reveal itself in them.

After the 12:12 a transition through dimensional opening of the 11:11 into the world of Oneness carried on. The actual transition of your Planet into higher dimension commenced. Earth will become a sacred Planet. It means lifting of its physical matter towards etheric plane. On etheric plane a new Earth will become, a planet of Oneness, in total alignment with the New Heaven through the revelation of no-time and no-space.

This transition process of matter into higher dimension will begin in Conversion vortices, which began to be activated around the time of 12:12 activation. Conversion vortices are energetic vortices of liquid Light, which enable the transition of energies from the world of duality into Oneness. They are oases of the new reality. Starry stones can serve as centers of Conversion vortices in your physical world.

Dimensional door of 12:12 triggered the process through which some spiritual groups will become Conversion vortices, as well as some power spots on your world. Islands of Light which you will create will serve as Conversion vortices as well.

In Conversion vortices those of you who will decide for transition in the world of Oneness will become slowly invisible for those from the world of duality. This will occur at the moment when your consciousness will be completely anchored in the world of Oneness. At that moment matter of your body can for some time be lifted towards the etheric plane. Each Conversion vortex will have its spiritual quality; it will be acting on a certain ray. Conversion vortices will be connecting together into a Light grid, called Antarion grid. Purpose of STAR PEOPLE on Earth is that through the establishing of Antarion Light grid they raise the vibration of this planet and assist it on its way into the higher dimension. Each phase of this grid will be established completely by activation of every gate of the dimensional opening of the 11:11. This will accelerate the growth of humanity very much. Extraordinary inflow of energies through the Antarion grid will create a sudden shift of whole Earth towards the etheric plane at the closing of 11:11. At that time energy from the Galactic Central Sun will come directly towards Earth. At that moment the last remnant of the astral cloud, which has surrounded Earth before will be removed. Ascended Masters who will gather in the Wesak Valley at the sacred mountain Kailas in Tibet will make a final anchoring in the spiral of Oneness. That moment means the birth of New Earth and completion of the Antarion conversion. And path home, into the Galactic Oneness, will be open and sparkling as never...

ASHTAR COMMAND KROTRON STARBASE
IXATAAR INTERCEPT 12:21
END OF TRANSMISSION

---

# UNCONDITIONAL REDEMPTION

We have paid off all debts. We have awakened Divine spark in our hearts. The Light of redemption has come.

Hello, divine sparks, flames of One. I am Krotron Antarion. This is the Ashtar Command, Krotron StarBase. We are with you and you are with us to travel together into the New reality, which is revealing in front of us.

You are the One, dear Starry Angels that have enabled the revelation of that New reality in this Galactic sector. Long time ago you have made your decision to incarnate in worlds of Local Logos. You have enabled by that the raising of the vibration of matter of those worlds. Your existence in zone of Star gates of the Local logos allowed its current transition into the world of Oneness, so that Local logos is serving now as a transformational point for enormous parts of Galaxy, along with some other zones in this Galaxy it contributes to the completion of the Galactic network of Light and manifesting New reality.

When you incarnated in matter, you have accepted your decision to experience duality. You have done that by cutting yourself from the source of One, cutting yourself from the Divine spark and you have shifted from the law of the Divine Grace into the law of karma. Because the experiment of duality is now completing in this Galactic sector, this means unconditional transition back again from the law of karma into the law of Divine Grace.

The 12:12 activation brought termination of status of forbidden area for this planet. Vibration of this planet is now high enough to start the process of acceptance in the Galactic confederation. This will undoubtedly trigger an intense increase of visits of extraterrestrial beings to your world. After the 12:12 activation Lord Sananda, whom you call Christ, began to transmute all karma that you surrender to him. This heralds the beginning of unconditional redemption, which will be happening with great acceleration, in next years.

This planet goes towards its unconditional redemption. This is the Divine Plan, this is its destiny. And all life beings who will remain on this planet will be redempted as well. Those who will not wish to be redempted, who would like to continue with karma, will be evacuated to some other planets, which will allow that form of life. Unconditional redemption is beginning to happen right now when Earth is entering an inner section of ring of Light. This is a zone of increased presence of One, which is bringing the vibration of Oneness, Light, deliverance and divine Grace in the matter of your planet. It is a zone of direct presence of the Galactic logos, of the consciousness of the Galactic Sun, which is now softly surrounding your solar system and your planet.

Along with that your planet entered the Photon Belt. The Photon Belt is the fifth dimensional belt of vibration of liquid Light, which surrounds the Local Central Sun, the star Alcyone in Pleiades. This belt is intersecting the orbits of star systems of the Local logos, which are gathered around the Pleiades. Your Sun does one circle around the Local Central Sun in 25.800 years and on its way intersects the area of the Photon Belt twice. A transition though the zone of increased energy takes about 2000 years each time. Last such transition happened at the final deluge of Atlantis. The next one is happening now. The vibrational frequency of your planet is increasing dramatically and will remain increased. This will mostly likely cause some chaos in your energetic systems, in your technology, but as a result of this, your consciousness will be expanded beautifully.

The first and the second wave of Ascension are actually a preliminary for the final redemption of mankind, which will happen at the third wave. Some rare individuals will be ascended even before the first wave. The first wave is right ahead of us. This is the current estimate which can still change somewhat. The minimum number of volunteers who are needed for the first wave is about 700. If the first wave of Ascension occurs to soon there are not enough Ascended Masters volunteers returning to Earth. If it occurs too late there is not enough time to prepare the second and the third wave. So therefore we try to catch the optimum moment which will have the maximum effect on the benefit of the whole humanity. Some days or some hours before Ascension we will increase the intensity of the vibration of the ascension column dramatically. This column is already surrounding your bodies. The energy of liquid Light will assist you to align with the vibration of the Ascension and this will cause your lifting upon the levitation beam in our ships. Although the actual lifting will occur at a certain moment in the near future, the Ascension process is already taking place in your heart. You do not need to put Ascension in your future. Ascension is happening now.

The Ascended Masters of the first and the second wave will prepare everything for the final redemption at the third wave. Then Light of Oneness will surround Earth. Anybody who would choose that will be redempted. Regardless of what he did in his past, everybody carries the Divine spark in his heart. And Divine spark of all humanity accepted decision for unconditional redemption. All karma will be miraculously and instantaneously transformed and absorbed into consciousness of One.

This will be the final liberation of your Solar system. By the year 2012 of your time, Dark Lords of Orion will be completely removed from Earth, which will enter the vibration of Oneness. At that time Archangel Metatron will close the dimensional opening of the 11:11, in the Star gate of AN. This will be a completion of unconditional redemption...

ASHTAR COMMAND KROTRON STARBASE
INTERSECTION 11:11:83/12:21
END OF TRANSMISSION

# TECHNOLOGY OF REDEMPTION

And so the fabric of New reality is emerging, invisible field of consciousness, which surrounds Earth and changes it in a point of Light inside the Galactic network of Light ...

Hello, Divine sparks, flames of One. This is the Ashtar Command, Krotron StarBase. We are with you and you are with us to travel together in the New reality, in the New Heaven and in the New Earth. The old reality will be redempted and miraculously transformed. Technology of redemption is a technology of activation of the morphogenetic field of presence of Conversion vortices. Morphogenetic field is an energetic grid, in which consciousness of One is present. Conversion vortices are vortices of a presence of One, which instantaneously and miraculously transform the creations of the spiral of duality and absorb them into One. A change from Duality into Oneness occurs through the process of triangulation.

Triangulation is a process of dis-identifying from mental states of duality and their transcendence. Every mental state of duality has its opposition. By alternatively going deeper with your consciousness in such pair of states you get dis-identified from them and achieve synthesis on a higher plane. You can gradually transcend the whole mental world of the spiral of duality, and when a change on the mental level is created it soon causes a change in your emotions and also in your physical world. Triangulation occurs spontaneously by itself, if you constantly surrender all aspects of your life to Oneness.

Therefore Conversion vortices are instrument of Divine intervention, which transforms the law of manifestation, the law of karma, into the law of Divine Grace. Conversion vortices bore presence of Miraculous into the third and forth dimensional structure of reality of duality. When a critical mass of a presence of Miraculous is attained, a structure of reality changes and a quantum shift into fifth dimension occurs.

## GROUPS OF ASCENSION

Those of you who decide for the first or the second wave of Ascension are the pioneers of redemption for this Planet. You are those who will create the Antarion grid. Time has come when you can begin to establish Ascension groups. Those groups will be a physical manifestation of Conversion vortices. It would be wonderful if such groups were created all over the country not only in bigger cities. So the Light grid will emerge. Those of you, who feel a call, to create such groups, will be given exact instructions. Find a place where you can meet once a week, each week at the same time spot, at the same day, at the same hour. So an energetic cycle will be generated which will strengthen the connections between you and us. By establishing group of Ascension it is not important how many of you gather together. Even if you are alone, insist, dedicate to this work once a week and soon enough energy will be generated and others will come also. It is important for you to dare to express what you feel to those in your surroundings who might understand you. Also ask us for assistance and support by establishing this group. Each group needs to have its own Starry stone, a Moldavite or tektite which will act as an anchor of the presence of Oneness. You can surround it with a pyramid that will create an interdimensional window though which Miraculous will reveal itself. Through this stone we will send you energy of Oneness, which will align the whole group.

Conversion vortex is a six dimensional Angelic being, which attracts manifestation of the New reality. It causes gathering of the soul families in Ascension groups, in Islands of Light and accelerates their Ascension. In the physical world it represents the anchoring of the New reality through clear relationships of Angelic beings inside the soul family. You have transcended a need for learning through relationships, which are not based on truth. Release those relationships from your life.

Better relationships will come, through which you will learn Love. When you create your Ascension group, meditate together, talk to each other, spread Love, touch each other, caress each other, and merge together. Liquid Light will blend all of your energies into pulsating vibrations of Light, color, shape, sound and cause the beginning of transition of your consciousness into the New reality.

Multi dimensional consciousness of no-time and no-space will begin to reveal itself, a zone where your and our consciousness meet and merge into One.

We are giving you technology for establishing Conversion vortices. You can use that each time when the group meets. At this sacred work we shall really be with you.

Instructions follow: Members of a group make a circle. Raise your hands above your head and begin to rotate on a spot clockwise. Vibrate a mantra iiiii, so that your whole body is vibrating in this sound. Imagine that your body is transforming into a brilliant white pillar of light, powdered with rainbow stars, into the vortex of Ascension. Through some time stop rotating and visualize that this column is rotating inside of you. With this you will magnetize our consciousness that it will merge with yours and anchor in your body. Then begin to rotate again, time with your hands dropped. Imagine a spiral vortex of rainbow Light, which is expanding from your heart throughout the world in a horizontal plane. Vibrate mantra eeaaaa, so that with the whole body you vibrate in this sound. It will call your soul family, soul mates and twin soul. Imagine how they join you in this rotation. When you feel you can stop and go into meditation. Exciting journey into worlds of Oneness is beginning. We are with you, Angels are with you, beings of Light also. Sacred dreams are becoming true for you and for us.

ASHTAR COMMAND KROTRON STARBASE
IXATAAR INTERCEPT 11:11
END OF TRANSMISSION

# CHANGES ARE COMING

And seven veils will be unveiled, one after the other, until the Only Sun is revealed.

Hello, Divine sparks, flames of One. I am Azaris RaMu.This is the Ashtar command, Krotron StarBase. We are with you and you are with us to unveil together the veils of space and time and to merge with Oneness, which is revealing beyond them.

Seven seals of revelation will unseal the seven Cosmic doorways of consciousness. The first seal is represented by Star gate, which was opened on the 25th of May 1975 and enabled the disciples of Ascended Masters access to certain parts of Divine Plan which enables the healing of mankind. The second seal is a doorway of Harmonic convergence, which was opened on the 16th and 17th of August 1987 and allowed the anchoring of the fourth dimension. The third seal is represented by the first gate of 11:11, which opened on the 11th of January 1992 and allowed anchoring of the fifth dimension. And this was the beginning of entrance into the world of Oneness. The fourth seal is represented by the second gate of the 11:11, which opened on the 5th of June 1993. It allowed anchoring of the sixth dimension and revelation of the sphere of Cosmic Love.

This started a process of creating of Conversion vortices, rainbow spiral whirlpools of Ascension. The fifth seal is the doorway of the 12:12, which represents the completion of the forth dimension and point of transition from the zone of karma in the zone of Divine Grace. The sixth seal is represented by the third gate of the 11:11, which anchored the octave seven and this will help establishing the Light grid, a grid of

Conversion vortices. The seventh seal of revelation is represented by the Antarion doorway, which opened on the 11th of August 1999 and represents the turning point of transition in the world of Oneness. Seven seals of revelation represent seven steps in the process of initiation of this Planet.

## YOU ARE ENTERING A CREATION OF LIGHT

After the 12:12 activation onwards, the transition into the world of Oneness is accelerating fast. From November 1994 on the Ashtar Command is more actively present with its energies in your world. After the 12:12 activation, the vibration of your Planet is raising fast. The raising of the vibrational frequency will cause many changes in your world. Small groups of Ascension will begin to be established. Those groups will receive the energy of liquid Light, of different energetic rays, coming from the Galactic Central Sun through the Polar Star and then through various Star gates of the Local logos towards your planet. Those who are on the Ascension path will experience the awakening of the One eye. The One eye is not a chakra, it is a psychic organ, eye of vision, with which you can see in the invisible worlds. Entrance in a new state of consciousness will enable you to raise your vibration of your physical body in your Light body, which glows inside with its own Light. Then you will be able to see the Miraculous world, a world of beauty. In those moments you can become slowly invisible for your surrounding, because you will shift in the etheric spiral of Oneness, which is not visible for the world of duality. When you achieve a totally clear consciousness in the world of Oneness, many miracles reveal to you. You will learn that as a being of Light, you can create and shape your physical world. A time has come for you, when you will create consciously your life. Reality is aligning with your decisions. As you decide, so it is. When you decide, a change in the mental word has already happened. You need only to wait for some time for it to manifest in the physical world as well. You are the one who creates. You are not slaves to Natural laws. You are the law itself, divine Light in your heart is Natural law itself. Allow the dreams of your heart to live and fly. Life is full of unexpected changes, which guide you in the right direction. Ask for support. Ask Angels, beings of Light, Ascended Masters, Starry brothers. Ask for help and it will be received thousand times. Everything that you wish can be done. Make your decision, make your first step and insist in asking for our support. We can help you much more than you think. Open your heart towards gratefulness. Surround with gratefulness all good that you receive and you will receive more. And so Light will spread in your heart. If you are in troubles, do not be desperate. You are not victims of the world that you see. That what is not aligned with your heart, you can release from your life. Darkness which you forgive does not last long. It changes into the Light. So do not be afraid. Be brave, be what you are. Express that outwards. In your life you can namely attract only that what you express outwards. We are with you and support you.

In 1975 it became possible for us to represent the Plan of the Ascension waves to some disciples of the Ascended Masters. Some individuals have ascended from that time already. Some Star beings are right now in intensive preparations to be ascended even before the first wave. A great majority of you are preparing for the first or second wave. In the next following years you will experience completion of your spiritual growth, your final liberation. There will be also great changes in the external world. Prepare for those changes peacefully, firmly and with Love. And we are with you ...

ASHTAR COMMAND KROTRON STARBASE
IXATAAR INTERCEPT 11:11
END OF TRANSMISSION

---

# CREATION OF UNIVERSES

He is collecting burning dust. He will create Suns, Universes, worlds ...

Hello, Divine sparks, sons and daughters of One. I am Krotron AntariOn. This is the Ashtar Command, Krotron StarBase. We are with you and you are with us to merge, that spirit and matter become One again.

Cosmic Consciousness of One is separating from itself and in the dance of Creation it creates Universes. Created Universes are reflected pictures in which One can see itself and know itself. New Universes grow from the existent ones through dimensional opening of black/white holes, they are like bubbles of densified Light on a membrane of Cosmic space-time, which expands and contracts. When purpose of those Universes is completed, they are ascended back into One through Divine intervention. With realizations, which One has achieved through their existence, its consciousness in enriched. Consciousness of One, which manifests, is namely not perfect yet, and is still developing through Cosmic cycles, through Cosmic in breaths and out breaths. In the first attempts of Creation, Cosmic consciousness has not succeeded in creating balance between spirit and matter. So in the past, some Universes were too rigid and they have blocked the evolution too much, others were overly dispersed and had not enabled the focusing of consciousness, through which the evolution is taking place.

Only in the current, sixth Cosmic cycle, satisfying balance between spirit and matter was achieved. This enabled quick development and now after twenty billion years this Cosmic Cycle is completing through the revelation of dimensional doorway of the 11:11. Ascension of Cosmos through the dimensional doorway of the 11:11 will enrich the Cosmic consciousness of One, with realizations of all beings who were participating in the life wave of this Cosmic cycle. Until now, the consciousness of One allowed life beings to develop in alignment with their freewill, but it has not given to them the possibility of unconditional redemption, if they would go too far with their freewill. Now the Cosmic consciousness of One is realizing through the experiences of all beings that are part of its consciousness, that every living being, along with it freewill needs also a possibility of redemption. This is now happening and so in this Cosmic cycle, the first unconditional Ascension on a Cosmic scale will happen. Ascension means converging different possibilities into One. As many Galaxies, Suns, planets and civilizations Ascend, less and less possible Universes remain. Universes fulfill their purposes one by one and return into One. At the end, in the last Cosmic cycle, the last one will remain. This will be the Perfect Universe. At that time the consciousness of One will look at itself in a perfect mirror and the last Universe will be Ascended. This will mean the end of Cosmic time and space, only eternal no-space and no-time in One will remain. The purpose of Creation will be completed. Cosmic consciousness will know itself completely.

## DENSIFICATION OF THE LIQUID LIGHT

Spirit and matter are aspects of One. Matter is created as a child of Divine tantric marriage of spirit with itself, through birth of Cosmis space and time. It is created as a densification of the liquid Light, as merger of beloved Cosmic Shiva and Cosmic Shakti. Liquid Light creates different dimensions and planes of existence through various levels of densification. It creates a spiral of Oneness and by further densification a zone of overlap, called the 11:11, is created and when the liquid Light condenses completely into matter, a spiral of duality is created.

Unmanifested beingness, absolute Oneness as Cosmic nothing, called An (One), lives outside Cosmic space and time. It only is. Nothing more can be said about it.

In amazing transition, which is a higher octave of dimensional opening of the 11:11, One directs itself into the abstract manifestation of absolute, into Cosmic all, which you call An Sof (a curtain of One). This is Cosmic divine essence, source of all that is, source of the spiral of Oneness. Therefrom a Cosmic divine spark is developed, a Cosmic sphere of light which you call An Sof Aur (light of the curtain of One). From Cosmic Divine spark a Cosmic egg is developed which is the seed of all Creation. It is a Divine will for a Creation, a Cosmic consciousness that you call Shiva. When the force of Creation begins to densify the Cosmic Light, Cosmic consciousness begins to separate from itself. One begins to separate on Cosmic Shiva and Cosmic Shakti. This is a consciousness of Cosmic Love, called Vishnu, which maintains Cosmic balance. This is a zone of consciousness of Galactic logoi, beings who manifest through whole Galaxies. With further densification of Cosmic Light, the Cosmic mind that you call Brahma is created, which creates essence of Divine Plan for Creation. This is a zone of consciousness of Solar logoi, beings who manifest through Stars. When Divine Plan is created, a wish for Creation appears. This is a zone beyond unknown, when we are already entering an overlap between the spiral of Oneness and the spiral of duality, which is called the 11:11. This is a zone of the consciousness of the sons of One, seeders of the worlds, planetary logoi, called Elohim. These are mighty Angelic beings who create Cosmos with densifying basic atoms of Creation from the essence of Cosmic Light. Cosmos is created in areas of dimensional doorways called EL AN RA, which are spread throughout all important time-space points.

Basic atoms of pure Creation are created from Cosmic Light, Cosmic sea of Divine sparks, from which beings with individual consciousness will be created. This is a zone of octave eleven, a zone of Archangel consciousness. In octave eleven Cosmic Light splits on twelve rays. Each of them is a bearer of one of the qualities of Cosmic Light. The first ray brings energy of purpose, the second ray energy of love and wisdom, the third ray the energy of creativity, the fourth ray the energy of synthesis, the fifth ray the energy of knowledge, the sixth ray the energy of devotion and the seventh ray the energy of manifestation. The higher rays bring higher dimensional energies that are almost inexistent on this planet. Through various combinations of energies of those rays, the variety of all forms of Cosmos is manifested. So the liquid Light densifies further through rays and the octave seven is created, where there is a home of all Divine sparks of all beings. This is a state of consciousness of Ascended Masters, a consciousness of Divine purpose. Masters are One in their consciousness, your idea clothes them with form so that you can discern them one from another. In octave seven the zone of overlap between the spiral of Oneness and spiral of duality, called the 11:11 is ended. When liquid Light densifies even further we are already in the zone of spiral of duality, in the zone of sixth dimension. Here spirit and matter do not reveal together as One anymore, but they seem to be separated. Sixth dimension is the zone of unconditional Love, zone of intuition. Liquid Light then densifies into the fifth dimension, which is the zone of soul consciousness. It's an area where insight into all times and spaces is possible, a world of illuminated mind, Heavenly world of Light. When liquid Light densifies even more, concrete forms begin to be created from Divine fifth dimensional archetypes. Here the real duality begins, linear space and time are created. Mental forms of duality densify even more and surround themselves with emotional (astral) matter. This is a zone of fourth dimension. Liquid Light condenses even further; it surrounds itself with etheric matter, which your physicists would call ionized plasmatic cloud. It densifies even more, from atomic cores of etheric plane physical atoms that represent physical matter in its gaseous, liquid and solid dimensional state are created. So the third dimension is reached, the lowest point, which matter can reach. And when matter carries out its purpose in the physical world, it is ascended back to etheric plane through the Light tunnel (dimensional window) and then through eon's of time and no-time it raises its vibration through dimensional doorways, until sometime each Divine atom will come back to its source. And at that time Everything will be completed...

ASHTAR COMMAND KROTRON STARBASE
ISIS INTERCEPT 11:11
END OF TRANSMISSION

---

# ABOUT TWIN SOULS

At the beginning of time, dance began. Two souls, spirally getting closer to each other. This is the eternal dance of One heart ...

Hello, Divine sparks, daughters and sons of One. I am Krotron AntariOn. This is the Ashtar Command, Krotron StarBase. We are with you and you are with us to travel together in the Galactic Oneness. As Starry family of Divine sparks, we have all been created inside the Galactic Central Sun, called Alfa and Omega, in Starry language Alohae An Aloha, in the zone of octave seven. Actually all our Divine sparks are only one Divine spark, one and only seven dimensional permanent atom. So in octave seven everybody is One with the whole life. Starry family then traveled throughout the Galaxies, in different directions as Angelic host inside octave seven. In a zone of dimensional doorways of the Local logos, such as Sirius and Alcyone, it lowered its vibration of frequency in six dimension and so group souls were created. Group souls are six dimensional permanent atoms, which are projection of the only Divine spark into sixth dimension. Group souls were taking part in the Cosmic evolution in the area of dimensional doorways of the Local logos and they have attained their first Ascension there. Group soul, which attained its first Ascension in Pleiades is called AnNutTaRa, in star language. Ascended Divine sparks of group souls have scattered in various Star systems inside the Local logos, after the Ascension. Most of them have decided to cooperate in the experiment of duality, at the end of which they will go now in the second Ascension. Those souls which have decided to enter the world of duality lowered their vibration in the zone of fifth dimension. Six dimensional permanent atoms have scattered into fifth dimensional ones. Each soul, each fifth dimensional permanent atom, created two rainbow interwoven bodies of Light, two twin souls. Fifth dimensional permanent atom split on two half's, of which one is male and the other is female. By rotating around its axis the fifth dimensional permanent atom began to create space and time and thus enabled entrance in the world of duality. Each of twin souls began then to incarnate on various planets, followed its own spiritual path and acquired experiences in the world of duality, but both were always connected on all planes of existence, except on physical one. Now the experiment of duality is completing. This means meeting of all Divine sparks of the Starry family, meeting of soul mates and twin souls. We shall create together a Starry Mandala which will allow us to travel in the evolution of Oneness through the Star gate of An. As one being we will travel inside the dimensional axis of the 11:11:83 into the consciousness of the Galactic Central Sun. Dimensional axis of the 11:11:83 is the anchor of Oneness of the dimensional doorway of the 11:11. It was anchored on Earth by 83 participants of the second gate activation of the 11:11. This allowed meeting of Starry family, especially soul mates and twin souls, in the consciousness of Oneness. Those meetings will be occurring more and more until the closing of 11:11, when all the Starry family will be finally gathered together and every Star being will meet its twin soul. Energy of Oneness will bring all together through magnetic attraction. Each Star being among you creates namely a rainbow vortex of magnetic attraction. This is a vortex of your Angelic presence which activates when you open your One eye and One heart. Before you will meet your twin souls, you will begin to meet your soul mates. These are beings of Light, who are a part of the group soul that you belong to. In this lifetime they have incarnated in the bodies of opposite sex, so you can create together fulfilling love relationships. Magnetic attraction rules among you, a feeling of closeness, a feeling of being at home. Those relationships will prepare you for the twin soul relationship which is very intense. Relationship with the twin soul heralds the final completion of duality. Twin soul was meant for everybody of you in the Stars.

You will meet the twin soul because your Light body bears Star codes of the 11:11:83 inside of it and which enable such meeting. Meeting will happen when you are anchored firmly in Oneness, when your emotional body becomes a clear transmitter of Cosmic Love. Therefore this meeting usually happens in the last lifetime. In the moment of liberation, when you release your last judgments, when you become Light, your twin soul is always physically present. Therefore meetings of twin souls occur more often at the completion of Cosmic cycles, when many more beings attain liberation. Such meeting is always very intense. You will feel an intense energy, but closeness and relaxation at the same time. When this happen you will know that you met your twin soul. Even before physical meeting you can meet on internal planes, in your meditation or dreams. Your twin soul (which in Starry language is called MaNa), is your ideal mate, who is completely aligned and connected with you. It is your other self, your perfect mirror, a being of Light, who is your equal fellow traveler. The relationship with the twin soul is conscious Oneness on all levels of existence. In the area of octave seven, there is a Cosmic Oneness among you and together you can say : I am. In the zone sixth dimension you feel Cosmic Love and you can say: I am you and you are me. In the fifth dimension magnetic attraction rules among you and you can say: We are. In the area of fourth dimension you exchange energy through telepathy, communication and feelings. You allow expressing all mental and emotional energies; you talk about everything and allow all feelings. So you can say: We communicate and feel each other. In physical world, in third dimension, energy between you is flowing through touch and physical merger. And when you say: we are merging, Oneness finally manifests and expresses in all dimensions.

Your relationship is relationship of two Angelic beings, through which the Miraculous is revealed, where soul falls in love with beauty. This is the area where finite melts into Infinite, where everything visible disappears into Invisible. You both feel and know that you are One, you deepen into energies of Oneness until Infinite. Your relationship is a Cosmic merger, which brings among you perfect understanding and harmonic alignment. It allows healing of all wounds of the past; it enables you to see the best in each other and in yourself. It enables dramatic acceleration of the Ascension path for both, it allows you to carry out your common Divine mission much more easily and much more effectively. Therefore the Ascended Masters will bring you together at the optimal point. You dream the common dreams of Oneness. Your complementary characteristics allow you to learn together and so your dreams are coming true. And the rainbow spiral of Oneness begins to reveal among you and among the whole Starry family, among us and you.

ASHTAR COMMAND KROTRON STARBASE
ISIS INTERSECTION 11:11
END OF TRANSMISSION

---

## MEDITATION FOR CONNECTION WITH YOUR TWIN SOUL

Calm your thoughts, emotions and your physical body, and open your heart. Visualize a pillar of Light, which emanates from the Sky, goes through you and then onwards towards the centre of the Earth. Then visualize a spiral vortex of rainbow Light which emanates from your heart. Visualize this vortex expanding throughout the world and awakening and calling your twin soul. Visualize your twin soul in front of you as an ideal mate and open towards her energetic presence. Connect your chakras with chakras of your twin soul with etheric cords of liquid Light. You connect your crown chakra with the crown chakra of your twin soul with the energetic cord of violet color, you connect your brow chakra with the brow chakra of your twin soul with energetic cord of indigo color, you connect your third chakra with the cord of light blue color, you connect your heart centre with the cord of green color, you connect your solar plexus with yellow color, you connect the sacral centre with the cord of orange color and you connect the base centre with the cord of red color.

Look into the eyes of your twin soul and feel the connection with her on all planes of Creation. Let her presence surround you completely. Visualize yourself embracing her and merging with her in a kiss. Breathe together with her, and as you breathe in, surrender all of your yearnings towards your twin soul and when you breathe out accept yearnings of your twin soul in your heart. Feel the happiness of this merger. This happiness is the only thing that will remain in the world of Oneness.

When you would like to conclude the meditation, internalize this merger and imagine that it is happening inside of you. When we anchor this energy into our bodies we are creating a magnet which calls our twin soul into external world also.

# COMMUNICATION WITH THE KROTRON STARBASE I

We are publishing parts of communication with the Krotron StarBase, which occurred every Wednesday in the Ascension group in Ljubljana

* *Can you describe Krotron StarBase?*

"It is a complex of many Star ships. From our perspective it is actually a densified Light, a focused consciousness of our unified presence. If you looked with etheric sight you would see a complex of Star ships, some of them stationed some of them moving. Mother ship of the Krotron StarBase hovers above Ljubljana and is surrounded by smaller ships and UFOs which are carrying out their missions every day. Activity of Krotron StarBase is focused upon Slovenia. Our StarBase is in direct energetic and telepathic connection with the mother ship Excalibur and the whole Ashtar Command. In the core of each ship there is a Light pillar which is our energetic connection with the Galactic Central Sun. Mother ship of the Krotron StarBase is our home. Smaller ships serve as a connection between you and us, like for example StarBase which is currently merging with your group. Some bases are anchored above your homes if you are upon the Ascension path, if you express your wish to have permanent or temporary presence of StarBase above you. Some ships are intended for scientific-research work, some are working on creation of the Light grid, but above all they are dealing with spreading a presence of Love in Oneness in your world. "

* *What is Xertron and Tritron?*

"These are two remaining Star Bases above Slovenia. Xertron StarBase is anchored above Celje and Tritron StarBase is anchored above the Triglav National Park."

* *Why are Starry beings incarnating to unstarry parents?*
"Because of the lack of Starry parents. Starry beings are incarnating in generation waves. First of those intensive waves was in late fifties, the second one in between 1967 and 1975."

* *What is the role of Master St. Germain in connection with the karmic board?*
"Master St.Germain is the keeper of the violet flame which transmutes karma. He released a request for its use towards karmic board. This request was approved. Karmic board is currently amidst great changes, because there is an instruction from above for release of all karma, for change of all karmic notes in the akashic records. Experiment of duality is concluding and all the karma will be transmuted into the Light. So the function of the karmic board is slowly coming to an end."

* *In what bodies we lived on Sirius and Pleiades?*
"On Sirius you lived in etheric bodies of dolphinoid or humanoid shape and on Pleiades as Angelic beings in the Light bodies."

* *I have received the message that the first wave of Ascension will happen on 15th of April 1995. Is this true?*
"There will be very intense energies on that day. This is a possible time point for the first wave, like it was on the 12th of December 1994. Energies will be very strong, nearly as strong as at the 12:12 activation. This is not yet the optimum point for the first wave is a possible point. But we are giving no guarantees that the first wave will happen then."

* *I would like to begin to channel . How can I do that?*
'First get your Starry name. Then you can write down on a piece of paper: I am and your Starry name. And then you write down in the name of your Starry Angelic presence whatever comes to

your mind. If you do that regularly for some time, you will discover that chaos slowly clears and sensible messages come out. When you have a firm and clear connection with your Angelic presence, with your soul, you can begin to communicate with us. Then you can write down on a piece of paper, for example: I am Krotron and write down your thoughts in a relaxed state. Through some time clear and sensible messages will come through, which will be a consequence of merger between your Angelic presence with our presence. When a strong link is established you can begin to test the messages in concrete life situations. Soon you will not need paper any more and you will be able to communicate with us in all situations".

* *How time will disappear?*

'Linear time, as you know, is a creation of your mind, illusion of the world of duality. Simply you will cease to create it. If you stop your thoughts, you stop time. And it will disappear. Your perception will change. The mind which creates time will fall away. Any by that time will fall away also. Ascension means transcending the mental world and the linear time. It means disappearing of the substance of the space-time continuum because of the expansion of the presence of Oneness. Time begins to contract and disappears at a certain point. Space begins to expand and at a certain point it disappears. Omnipresence of eternity occurs."

* *Why Am I so confused and irritated lately?*

"There is a cleansing of your emotional body taking place which you can not avoid. Because of the raising of your vibrational frequency all suppressed emotions come to the surface that you can release them with love and consciousness. So you heal yourself and help transforming emotions of the whole humanity. Through healing of your emotional bodies you will prepare yourselves for your Divine missions. Confusion in you will cease when you will feel that the Divine Plan is manifesting through you. People around you will be confused, but you will become pillars of stability amidst the chaos of the world, you will emanate Love and Oneness. Prepare yourselves. You will need to act efficiently. We can not act in your world otherwise than through you. You will receive visions that you begin to manifest now. And they will be manifested. Be awake. Time is running out. Prepare yourselves for migrations into the islands of Light. Prepare yourselves for living in Oneness

KROTRON ANTARION

# COMMUNICATION WITH THE KROTRON STARBASE II

* *In what way the law of karma will be transcended?*
"Everybody among you creates his own reality with own beliefs, thoughts, feelings and deeds. It is not the law of punishment, not even a law of Cosmic equilibrium. Cosmic equilibrium is always present. It is about you creating your reality in this moment. It is not about the consequences of the past deeds. Past and future are illusions of the mind of duality. Everything occurs in eternal moment as a multidimensional manifestation of One reality. With your decision you can transfer your attention from one to the other lifetime. Your are locking your experiences in your mind and thus you create your illusionary past, you are entangling yourselves in the net of your mind, you believe that you are guilty, you judge yourselves and you are creating realities in which you can pay off illusory debts. There is no external judge who would decide what you need to experience. Transcending karma begins with you realizing that you create your own reality. And when you know that you are innocent Divine beings of Light, you begin to forgive yourselves those illusory debts and you are thus entering the zone of Divine grace. And then as being of Light you create Divine reality spontaneously. This transition is occurring step by step. Activations of Star gates allow you to make these decisions easier and forgive yourselves."

* *How can I love in that man-woman relationship without being attached?*
"The first step is also self love. Then a flow of love begins to flow through you which attracts you towards those beings who are harmonically connected with you. Each of you creates a

vortex of Ascension. This means new interpersonal relationships. It means that you are not attached towards one particular relationship, but you create a Mandala of Ascension from many relationships, also man-woman relationships. So possessiveness, jealousy and emotional attachment will go away. And clearer and clearer Love will replace them."

* *How a process of healing of sexuality occurs?*

"A process of healing of sexuality occurs through expressing the sexual energy with an open heart. Each suppressed energy needs to be expressed though consciousness in order to be healed. Pain of many of you is a pain of separation between Love and sexuality. This pain is healing itself through merging energies of Love and sexuality in the Ascension mandalas, through group process of discovering of joy of merger of both energies. Both energies will merge into a new energy, into energy of Cosmic Love. This energy will spread itself through the energetic centre of Oneness, which is located about an inch above solar plexus center. This chakra is called the Galactic core and leads in the Galactic evolution of Oneness. "

* *In my brow chakra I see often bright shapes and my ears are ringing.*

*What does that mean?*

"In the transition into the fifth and higher dimensions the vibration frequency of your bodies is increasing. This causes various symptoms like whistling in ears, tiredness, pains in certain part of the body, fever, high temperature ... This is occurring to many of you. We recommend that you communicate about that towards each other and support each other. Light effects in the brow chakra are consequence of our cooperation with you. With energetic rays we are acting upon Star codes which are situated in this chakra and we activate them. As a result of this your consciousness is expanded and this is accompanied with various Light effects in this chakra. "

* *Can you see what is happening with us?*

"We can feel your vibration, but we do not see your world from your third dimensional perspective. We can see your world only when you invite us with your freewill to merge with your consciousness and look through your eyes and so together we can create the whole picture. We can receive a general impression about your physical body, but not concrete symptoms, except when you allow us to probe your body. Then we can discover energetic blockages, mental patterns, and the vibration in which you are existing and find the cause. And if you wish we can send you healing energies then. We are perfecting also the vibration of your emotional and mental body. It is important for you to talk to us in your thoughts and say to us what is happening to you. So we will cooperate with you and help you much easier. "

* *How can we collect money for the Island of Light?*
"You will become transmitters of huge quantities of money through the process of learning of perfect manifestation of the Divine Plan. You will learn to raise your vibration through group cooperation. In the world of duality competitiveness ruled among groups, and conflicts and control also. You will cooperate harmoniously. You will become aware of new way of manifestation through joyous creation. You will create an energetic vortex which will become magnet for money. Small and great miracles will happen. "

* *How can I manifest what I want?*
First make your unconditional decision what do you want and insist in this decision to fulfill your wish. Whenever doubts appear just renew your decision. The second step is to ask beings of Light and Angels for help in manifestation of your wish. Pour all your emotional energy that you have in this request. The last step is to act joyously and spontaneously outwards in the direction of manifestation of your wish and be open towards actual manifestation. If this manifestation does not occur immediately, just insist in repeating all three steps, because in your world the process of manifestation is occurring

with a certain delay often. We do not see any reason why you would not succeed, because you live in times when everything is possible. "

KROTRON
ANTARION

---

# ORDER OF THE STAR

And I have seen the New Heaven and New Earth, because former world has gone. And I have seen New Jerusalem coming from the sky.

Hello, Divine sparks, daughters and sons of One. I am Krotron AntariOn. This is the Ashtar Command, Krotron StarBase. We are with you and you are with us to look together where we came from, who we are and where are we going.

We will look at the journey of the core of the Starry family which consists of 144.000 beings of Light, 144.000 rainbow eagles. Many among you and many among us are rainbow eagles. Many millions years ago we entered the area of the Local logos through the Star gate An as the reconnaissance of the Angelic host of the whole Starry family, which consists of 11 millions beings of Light. Inside the An Star gate, Archangel Metatron awaited us and revealed individual divine mission to each of us. Then we have entered through the An Star gate in his presence through the glowing five-pointed star, which is created by five Creators of worlds who surround Metatron.

Then we descended together to Pleiades, on planet Ajaho. There we lived together in a perfect merger, in beautiful Oneness. This was the first Atlantis, called AlTa. Our group soul experienced its first Ascension there and received a name AnNutTara. Soon after that planet Ajaho exploded and Starry host moved onwards through the depths of space, towards Sirius. Sirius is the intermediary station, which prepared us for our mission which you and us carry out together on Earth. Under the guidance of the Dolphin king, called AQuaLa AWaLa in Star language, we were preparing in life in matter by surrounding our Angelic bodies of Light with etheric dolphin body. Joyfully and playfully we created dolphin vortices of merger through which we were realizing Oneness in matter.

When time came, most of the rainbow eagles went to Earth and some of them remained on Sirius and created the Blue Lodge of Sirius, which began to be involved in development of consciousness in Sirius and its near surroundings. Those of you and us who went on Earth, were involved in creation of the Ashtar and Jupiter Command and we represent its core, called the Eagelian Triad.

Jupiter command arranged its Star Bases around the twelve important Jupiter moons and so created a twelve fold Star which serves as an intermediary between the Blue Lodge of Sirius and Earth. Some of us have decided to remain on the ships. Some of you have decided to incarnate on Earth. You entered the Earth evolution in the times of Lemuria and Atlantis. In Atlantis you gathered together for the first time as Priests of White Star under the guidance of Merlin in the Danaan Land, which is today Ireland. This was just before the third Atlantian deluge. At that time a part of incarnated Star family decided to return to Pleiades, other part departed Atlantis and migrated towards East, and created a civilization in Asia, which is a forerunner of your present civilization. The third part remained in Atlantis and after the last wave of Star beings from Sirius came to Earth, Metatron gave instructions for establishment of the Order of the Star through the Blue Lodge of Sirius. In Dolphin temple in the city of Colardan many rainbow Eagles have gathered and created Order of the Star which purpose was to bring the experiment of duality to an end. Many of you were there. Lords of Fire from Shamballa handed over the Holy Grail in the hands of the Order of the Star. Holy Grail is a crystal chalice made of Moldavite, a symbol of the guardians of Oneness. As a part of the AnNutTaRa starry soul group you have incarnated together in various important periods of world history as guardians of the presence of Oneness and the Holy Grail migrated along with you. You were together in

Egypt, where you reestablished the connection with Sirius and established the Ascension temple in Luxor. You have gathered as disciples of Gautama Buddha as he attained his enlightenment. You were together as disciples of Jesus, gathered around the Apostles, who created the twelve fold Star of Ascension so that Jesus could achieve his liberation and show the way for the whole humanity. You were Knights in Britain, gathered around the twelve fold Star of Knights of the round table. You were tantrikas in Tibet where you have created the twelve fold stars of merger of Shiva and Shakti. And then in 1911 Krishnamurti revealed the Order of the Star to external world and prepared a way for the coming of New Atlantis.

## NEW ATLANTIS - NEW HEAVEN AND NEW EARTH

In this time AnNutTaRa starry group soul is incarnated in twelve sacred spots, which represent 12 chakras of the New Earth. These are the spots in which the second coming of Sananda is occurring. These are points in which group process of merger of consciousness in the vortices of Ascension is occurring. Those spots are transmitters of the presence of Oneness, which comes through the Ascended Masters and also directly through the Lords of Fire from Shamballa. Those points create a twelve fold Star of Ascension, the New Atlantis, a merge of New Heaven and New Earth. They form a basis of the Antarion grid, which will be built soon. We can reveal a position of six of those points. These are: Los Angeles, New York, London, Geneve, Muenchen and Ljubljana. Ljubljana has a special position among these points. Area of Ljubljana is the Antarion conversion for this Planet, this is an area of alchemical merger of Light of duality and darkness of duality into One. Area of European Community is a symbol for a planetary light of duality, when the area of the war in Bosnia is a symbol of the planetary darkness of duality. Slovenia is situated in a zone of overlap of both energies and creates a possibility for synthesis of both energies into the One. This land was chosen by the Galactic Confederation through Lords of fire from Shamballa for a conclusion of the experiment of duality. Therefore Shamballa protected it during the war some years ago and it will protect it in the future also. That land and Ljubljana especially, is the point wherefrom the consciousness of Oneness will spread in waves around the world. Also Ljubljana is becoming a magnetic vortex for repeated merger of the Order of the Star, and the Holy Grail will be brought to Ljubljana in the future. The symbol of Ljubljana vortex, which is a golden five pointed star on a dark blue basis, is namely also a symbol of the Order of the Star and the symbol of the King of the world Sanat Kumara from Shamballa. And through him the presence of Oneness will reveal, in the eye of the vortex, when the Antarion grid will be completed.

And through twelve fold star of Ascension, through rainbow vortices of Oneness, you will join us in the Ascended state. When the whole Earth will ascend, seven pathways will open for you. You could assist people who will choose duality and will be evacuated to other planets as Ascended Masters; you could remain on Earth as Ascended Masters of Oneness. You could work as being of Light inside the Ashtar or Jupiter Command; you could go to Sirius and join the Brotherhood of Og-min, the Blue Lodge of Sirius. There you could gather around the twelve fold star of the Council of twelve, who are representatives of the Galactic Confederation for the sector of the Local logos. You could act as intermediates between the Galactic Confederation and local civilizations around Sirius. You could travel onwards to Pleiades, where we will create together a planet, much more beautiful than Ajaho was. This will be New Alta, higher octave of New Atlantis. There some of us and you will live in perfect Oneness as Arch Angels. You could travel even onwards towards Orion, where you could assist in bringing energy of the One to this universe. You could travel even further, through dimensional door of An, beyond the unknown and join the Galactic evolution of Oneness as Creators of worlds. At these amazing opportunities you and we all become breathless...

ASHTAR COMMAND KROTRON STARBASE
ISIS INTERCEPT 11:11
END OF TRANSMISSION

# SACRED MERGER

At the end of time children of Light of all Star civilizations will dance the sacred spiral dance around the Galactic Central Sun. This will be a completion of the Galactic network of Light.

Greetings, brothers and sisters of Light. This is the Ashtar Command, mother ship Excalibur. I am Ashtar SherAn .I am with you now to issue you a call to the whole Starry family.

Long time ago you decided to enter the world of duality. When you have found yourselves there, you have suddenly felt separated from one another. And this triggered a yearning for reuniting inside of you. And this yearning is a magnetic force which will now merge you into the even deeper Oneness, it was the one at the beginning of time from where you entered duality. Now there is a time to reunite. So we are issuing the call to Starry family, which is gathering in your world in rainbow vortices of Oneness. Sacred merger is our purpose and it can be yours also. Because sacred merger of the sacred family is the path homewards, into Galactic Oneness.

Sacred merger begins inside of yourselves, when you begin to live in no time. When you stop your thoughts, for beauty of the Angelic presence to shine through silence. When you are one being, who has expanded its consciousness towards everything that is. Then you glow as a magnetic point of Light. And sacred merger goes on when you call your Star brothers and sisters with all your being to merge in one and only point of time and space. You call them to create with them closeness and sacred intimacy. You call your soul family to open your heart towards it, to merge with their souls and bodies as you were merging once on Sirius as dolphins. You call your soul mates to create deep relationships with them, which intertwine as rainbows. And you call your twin soul to merge with her in One being.

And every of your soul families becomes a point of Light in the Light grid. And Light grid is expanding and overflowing the world. This Light will soon overflow all areas of your world and lift it into the Heavenly world. Therefore it is important to connect all points of Light of your world in unified purpose. Each of your spiritual groups is a point of Light. A common purpose of all spiritual paths, which is Ascension, unites them. Ascension is the ultimate liberation of Man. Support in unified purpose and unify, cooperate in common projects and this will create a sacred merger of the whole Starry family. You are guardians of Oneness for this Planet. Merge together and act outwards as One being. In this way you will be able to spread Light and Love throughout the planet effectively. You are guardians of Oneness for this planet. You can not live as beings of duality and beings of Oneness simultaneously. In one point you are faced with the decision for the old or for the New world. Each of these worlds has its own natural laws and you can not live in a New world by the laws of the old one. When you enter the New world, cease all connections with the old one. All dependences from relationships based on duality, on fears, on jealousy, on compromises, all dependence on untruth. Take care of your happiness and do not allow inharmonic vibration to enter your life. Make your decision, wake up, because time is coming. You do not need to suffer any more. Remove the cause of suffering from your life and protect happiness which you will find afterwards. We are calling you, wake up.

ASHTAR COMMAND MOTHERSHIP EXCALIBUR
ISIS INTERCEPT 11:11
END OF TRANSMISSION

# WORLD LIGHT GRID

... and so the Light grid will be created, which will reveal the presence of no-time and no-space ...

Greetings, Divine sparks, daughters and sons of One. This is the Ashtar Command, Krotron StarBase. I am Krotron AntariOn. We are with you to give you instructions for establishment of the world network of Light.

Your world is in the period of transition into a new state of consciousness. Great inflow of energies which come to the world from depths of space, allow all beings of your world to become aware of everything that was once hidden. To lift all parts of their being in the Light of awareness and to merge them in whole with Love. This manifests in your world in different ways. On one side there is even clearer and clearer presence of the Light of One, and on the other side it is even sharper division of the world of duality. And when you are asking yourself if this humanity can save itself, you forget sometimes that the remedy is already there.

The rescue of your world lies in the establishment of the Light grid, which all of you create on your world, regardless of which nation you belong to, of which group, regardless of what you believe in, but there is sincere wish to bring more Light in this world which is uniting you. And you can find Oneness in this which transcends all differences of your belief systems.

And when a critical mass of you decides for Light and for the wish to help this world, you attain power to influence the occurrences in the world. At first only little, but then more and more and soon the power of your unified consciousness will make significant shift in your world, which will assist the Planetary

Ascension. Working in the triangle of the world network of Light is very simple and it takes only few minutes each day. Three people agree that they will connect in meditation each day or once a week on the same day to invoke the Light which would help humanity. So they are creating energetic triangle, which is a connection between the world of Oneness and humanity. You can perform this meditation each at your own time, you do not need to be aligned at the same moment. Because the world of Oneness which you are connecting with is beyond space and time. And if you would like you could also participate in more triangles. Each time you do that you enliven the substance of liquid Light, which circles your planet as a mantle. So the horizontal Light grid is created which will allow the lifting of your planet into the Ascended state .Each of your meditations is supported by meditations of the members of the Order of the Star, who act as intermediates between the Ascended Masters and the Light grid and create vertical vortices of connection between both worlds. Those vortices support the Light grid that you all can create. World network of Light is a field of liquid Light which will overflow the whole world. Everybody who feels a call can join it. And we are with you ...

## TRIANGLE MEDITATION FOR ESTABLISHING THE WORLD NETWORK OF LIGHT

1. Calm your mind and emotions and relax your physical body.

2. Align with both members of your triangle from the highest point of your consciousness and be aware of the triangle as the harmonious whole. Each time you think about it, you strengthen the energetic field of liquid Light.

3. Visualize your triangle as a part of the world network of Light.

4. Visualize light which flows in each point of your triangle. See Light circulating from point to point in triangle and then outwards through the network of Light into hearts and minds of all people. Then visualize that there is a sphere of pure consciousness which is a source of this Light.

More Light that you glow from the triangle outwards more flows through you so you can give it even more.

5. Loudly or in your mind speak the Great Invocation, which aligns your triangle with the world of Ascended Masters :

GREAT INVOCATION

From the point of Light within the mind of God
Let Light stream forth into the minds of men.
Let Light descend on Earth.

From the point of Love within the Heart of God
Let Love stream forth into the hearts of men.
May Christ return to Earth.

From the centre where the Will of God is known
Let purpose guide the little wills of men -
The purpose which the Masters know and serve.

From the centre which we call the race of men
Let the Plan of Love and Light work out
And may it seal the door where evil dwells.

Let Light and Love and Power
Restore the Plan on Earth.

# MER-KA-BA I

Ascension process is a process of change of the system of reality. And in your old system of reality of the third dimension, the body which was the bearer of your consciousness was your physical body.

In the new reality system in which you are entering, the body which will bear your consciousness will be your interdimensional Light body or Mer-ka-ba body. And your Light body is that body which allows your free transition from one into another dimension. It allows your activity in the third dimension, and it allows your activity in the fifth dimension, where you will have the ability and possibility of the interdimensional travel. Mer-ka-ba is an etheric-physical body, which is in direct connection with the seven dimensional body of Divine spark, which some of you call the atmic body. People of the Earthy evolution need to awake and develop this body; Star beings need only to renew connection with it.

In the days past the Angelic hosts of Star beings descended on Earth, on the Island of Mu in their fiery chariots, in their Light bodies. You were living there in the cities of Light close to Tahiti and close to Easter Island, which was called Rapa-Nui. This was the Garden of Eden. Split on two sexes and lowering the vibration of Star people meant exile from Eden. In Atlantis the connection with the atmic body was terminated by the use of implantation. Now the time has come for Star beings to renew this connection and re-activate their Mer-ka-ba.

First emotional cleansing needs to be done and connection with the Angelic presence needs to be established. Then the activation of One eye comes into place which expands Angelic consciousness. Your Angelic presence anchors in One eye and creates resonance field which increases the vibration of three dimensional physical and four dimensional astral and mental bodies. By the assistance of visualization you then prepare the mental form of Mer-ka-ba, which acts as a magnet for the consciousness of Divine spark. In a point of spiritual evolution, which some of you call the third initiation, Angelic consciousness is stabilized. Atmic body of Divine spark begins to influence the etheric-physical body through the mental form of Mer-ka-ba. The increasing connection with the consciousness of Divine spark transforms the physical body to raise its vibration into the fifth dimension. Genetic mutation of the DNA from twofold into twelve fold spiral occurs.

In the moment of Ascension the Divine spark lifts the vibration of the physical body to that extent that it merges with the etheric body. So an interdimensional Light body is created, with which you can travel in each dimension of space, time, no-space and no-time. Through dimensional doorway you can enter various Star systems. In this case your Mer-ka-ba body will serve as a space ship, as a StarBase.

## LUXOR POINT AND JOURNEY THROUGH THE 11:11

The anchor of the consciousness of the Divine spark is in One heart, in a special point inside the physical heart, which is called the Luxor point. This is a point of no-time, merger of the New Heaven and New Earth, the most sacred spot in the temple of human body. It is the anchor of the triple flame: the blue flame of Divine will, the rose flame of Divine Love and the golden flame of Divine Light.

Vibrations of love around the Luxor point creates electro-gravitational field of rays of liquid Light in the shape of flying saucer. Rotation of the rays of Light around this point with the speed of Light lifts the vibration of the physical body in etheric world and enables interdimensional travels and transition into the spiral of Oneness through the opening of the 11:11. Transition through the 11:11 began with the first gate activation which allowed the anchoring of the reality of the liquid Light. The second gate of the 11:11 allowed the beginning of the synthesis of the pairs of opposites. This process is called also triangulation. Before the third gate activation, namely in the years 1995 and 1996, entrance inside the Photon Belt occurred. This is a belt of five to seven dimensional liquid Light which spreads around the Local Central Sun Alcyone in Pleiades. This energy of Light and Love manifests only to a smaller extent in form of photons. Therefore it did not cause the catastrophic six days of darkness, as some people predicted. But it caused some chaos in your electronic systems. The purpose of the Photon Belt is above all in making the activation of Mer-ka-ba and Ascension easier.

Third gate of the 11:11 opened in 1997 and accelerated the establishment of Cosmic consciousness. Culmination of transition through the ring of Light of the 11:11, which needs not to be confused with the Photon Belt was at the fourth gate on the 11th of August 1999. The ring of Light emanates from the Galactic Central Sun and allows the planetary Ascension and activation of the planetary Mer-ka-ba body. This will ultimately create merger of the Starry family: a family of On (Star beings on space ships) and family of An (incarnated star beings). It will also cause extensive changes in this Solar system. Earth will become a planet of Love and will take over a role which Jupiter has now and Jupiter will become the New Sun.

From the activation of the fourth gate onwards the merger of the group Mer-ka-ba body of the whole Starry family inside the Local Logos began taking place. This will allow the Starry family to enter though the Star gate of An into the Galactic evolution of Oneness. We will be able to cooperate with the building of the Galactic Light grid in this and neighbor Galaxies. This will occur by the assistance of Star beings from M 31 Galaxy in Andromeda, which has already established Galactic Light grid and is the central Galaxy of the Local cluster of Galaxies. The other choice we would have is to enter through the Galactic Central Sun, in the zone beyond creation, into the unmanifested Cosmic Heart.

# MER-KA-BA II

The result of Mer-ka-ba body activation is the change of the system of reality. This will lead to many changes in your lives. Mer-ka-ba is the last teaching you can receive on Earth, all else you will be told by the Ascended Masters personally. At the Mer-ka-ba activation your consciousness rises towards the consciousness of Ascended Masters, quantum leap of consciousness occurs. These are sudden changes of consciousness. Universe has a quantum nature.

Evolution occurs through quantum leaps. Quantum leap occurs when a genetic shift occurs on a physical plane which is a consequence of a mutation of consciousness. Between old and new state of consciousness there is a narrow zone of chaos. Chaos is a state which allows you to call for redemption. Now processes occur very fast and are accelerating even further because of the changes of the structure of space - time continuum. Linear time is created by your mind, which is a part of the world of duality and when you cease to create time with your mind, everything can happen in a moment. The first consequences of the Mer-ka-ba activation are quantum leaps of consciousness. At the quantum leap you can over fly more steps in one single moment of no-time. Realization always comes in no-time.

When you activate your Mer-ka-ba you begin to see the substance of the spiral of Oneness. You begin to see the Star ships of the Ashtar Command and gradually you can see the invisible worlds, like the etheric or astral world. You can see this when you focus your consciousness in the void and not in the objects and energies. And you can see rainbow liquid Light everywhere.

At the Mer-ka-ba activation opening of the heart centre into One heart is also taking place. When this happens you can feel Love in every moment. Then you receive power of healing with Love and Light which works miracles. Miraculous healings can begin to occur. When your One heart opens you receive ability to levitate. Your physical body becomes lighter and is able to levitate, when the vibration of your physical body lifts towards the vibration of the etheric body. Etheric Light body has a certain weight, 0,1 gram, but you can neutralize this weight by the anti-gravitational electromagnetic fields of your Mer-ka-ba body. So you can walk upon water, float or fly through the air, and have the ability to transit in higher dimensions. The ability to levitate is activated from the fourth initiation onwards. A consequence of your Mer-ka-ba activation is also the ability of manifestation. In order to achieve that you need to open your Galactic core centre. You need to remove implant from that centre. Implants are crystals which block inflow of energies in various energetic centers. Mer-ka-ba is an interdimensional Light body and the oval of the Light body is an etheric form. First you need to create a mental form of this oval which manifests automatically towards the etheric plane. When we create a mental form, etheric matter gathers around it and so an etheric form is created. If we do not renew this form it decays. When this form is strong enough it attracts energy from the atmic body which also is oval in shape. By this we create connections between the atmic body and the mental form around which etheric matrix is created. The atmic body has a power to manifest and materialize. Then we can create a rainbow vortex which will magnetically call atoms which suit vibrationally to this etheric form which is inside of the oval. So we shape our desired manifestation in etheric form and place it inside our oval. This is a support field for manifestation, so called vortex support field (VSF).

When we rotate the rays of Light, the desired situation begins to manifest in the physical world. When the rays are rotating with the frequency of Love, which is equal to the speed of Light, an electro gravitation resonance field is created in the shape of flying saucer, which allows us to jump into the fifth dimension. In the spiral of Oneness, after the merger of consciousness of incarnated Star beings and Star beings upon the ships, after the merger of our Mer-ka-ba body with the Space ship of the Ashtar Command this energetic filed expands into the sphere of Light which is composed of fifth dimensional twelve fold Star. When the connection between the atmic body of the Divine spark and physical brain is awakened, you receive, step by step, the ability to materialize. When we master our Mer-ka-ba completely we can appear on many spots simultaneously.

Mer-ka-ba is an interdimensional body. If you project a spot from the fifth dimension into the third dimension you will get many spots. For understanding: a shadow of a third dimensional object is two dimensional, and projection of fifth dimensional object into the third dimension is a third dimensional one.

A permanent atom which belongs to us and our twin soul is one and the same thing in the fifth dimension. In physical world it is manifested in two physical bodies. So from a body of Light we can project in more physical bodies.

For the Mer-ka-ba activation vast changes in nutrition also take place. Heavy food becomes a burden, if you consume meat, give it up if it is possible. Do that gradually, without forcing yourself. Then you can begin to eat vegetarian food more and more, and slowly the need for food will fall off completely. Then you will feed yourself with etheric energy, which comes directly from Sun. And after that you will feed yourself with the substance of Oneness. It is very important to purify food. Food on earth is polluted energetically. You can purify food physically and energetically with violet flame. You can also bless food in the name of Lord Sananda.

After the third initiation onwards you become very sensitive and need to take care of the vibration of your physical body and the vibration of your surroundings. When your vibration is raised significantly above average, a great energetic tension is created. Then you become a magnet for darkness from your surroundings which would like to heal itself. More Light that you emanate, a greater magnet for darkness you become. It is important to purify your living space and you can also bless it with incense.

## GROUP MER-KA-BA ACTIVATION

Mer-ka-ba body can reflect outwards as a group relation of the soul family, soul mates and twin souls or as an Island of Light. Group Mer-ka-ba body is a StarBase, which surrounds the consciousness of the group soul, of a soul family, soul mates and twin souls. Twelve fold stars of the Light beings, together 144 beings, symbolically create such a StarBase.

Beings of a group soul gather and merge in vortices of Ascension. They activate those vortices by merging their Light bodies into One and merging their physical bodies into One. Vertical and horizontal merger occurs, a merger between each individual and his Light body into One, and merger of individual into a group Oneness. Merger into One being means perfect merger of all levels interdimensionally. This is a Divine marriage between Heaven and Earth. Extreme poles merge into One, a merger between spirit and matter occurs. Spirit is represented by atomic body whether the matter is represented by a physical body. Group Mer-ka-ba bodies activate when at least three of you gather together. For this activation a combination of One being in a male body, and more beings in female bodies is recommended.

Vortices of Ascension are energetic points upon this planet where New reality reveals itself. Inside those vortices dimensional doorway of the 11:11 can open before the scheduled time, because widening and contracting of space-time substance occur there and a redemption process also. This process is guided by the Angels of the Ascension vortices, so called Fire Angels. Those Angels transmute and remove implants by the use of the electric fire of redemption, and assist by the individual and group Mer-ka-ba activation. They accelerate the process of the group initiation in the world of Oneness, the group Ascension process. They are like great pumps that can absorb the whole group into the spiral of Oneness.

The Fire Angel of the Ljubljana vortex of Ascension is called IonaTaAn in the Starry language. Sanat Kumara transmits energy of redemption through this vortex. IonaTaAn was anchored in the centre of Ljubljana at the first gate of the 11:11 activation.

ASHTAR
COMMAND
ISIS
INTERSECTION 11:11

---

Technology for individual Mer-ka-ba activation was brought by Ascended Master Tehuti Bey. His twelve disciples create a twelve fold Star of Ascension which eases spreading of information about Mer-ka-ba outwards.

## MER-KA-BA ACTIVATION

The whole Mer-ka-ba activation technology can be transmitted only verbally or through telepathic communication. The first part of this technology can be written down and here it is for those who walk faster along the path of Ascension:

1. Visualize a being of Light, Ascended Master, which stands upon your head in his etheric body of Light, so that he touches your head with his feet.

2. Go into that being with your consciousness, identify completely with it and become that Master of Wisdom.
3. As an Ascended Master descend downwards again into your physical body and impregnate it with vibration of your Light body. By vibrating the sacred word OM and speaking your star name, if you know it.
4. Visualize that electric blue Light is emanating through all openings from your eyes, nose, and ears). This Light creates a magnetic field which calls your Angelic presence.
5. Cross your hands on your chest, so that the right hand covers your heart. Imagine that your heart is a source of warmth, which spreads around the body. Do that, vibrating the mantra Ka.
6. Spread your hands in the open position, inverted letter M. With this you spread the warmth through whole of your body. Do that, vibrating the mantra Lam.
7. Put your hands upon your head. Visualize a StarBase right above you which sends down the Ascension pillar right until the top of your head. Do that along with vibrating the mantra Ana.
8. Bring the ascension column down towards your feet with movement of your hands. Visualize it as a brilliant third dimensional oval of liquid Light, which surrounds your body. Do that along by vibrating the mantra On.
9. Purify your Mer-ka-ba body (the brilliant oval) with the violet flame which is rotating anti clockwise.

# MER-KA-BA III

The source of all knowledge of the Mer-ka-ba body is Archangel Metatron. He is transmitting this knowledge towards Earth by the use of the starry language of Light, by the use of harmonic waves of pulsating Light that travel through the great pyramid in Egypt into the twelve sacred spots on this Planet, which form a twelve fold Star of Ascension.

Knowledge about Mer-ka-ba is very important in this time, because it allows manifestation of Islands of Light. Islands of Light are external reflection of individual and group Light bodies. New relationships inside the Ascension groups allow the transition of consciousness into higher dimensions and as a result of this the manifestation of Islands of Light. Group merger of soul families allows the establishment of fifth dimensional field of liquid Light, deepening of the relationships with soul mates establishes a six dimensional field of Cosmic love and finally the merger with the twin soul in One being creates a seven dimensional field of Cosmic Oneness. Multidimensional merger creates a vortex of Ascension which is a vibrational buffer during the transition from the third into higher dimensions. It allows manifestation of five- to seven dimensional reality in physical world and therefore the creation of Islands of Light and finally group Ascension.

Islands of Light will be created mainly after the first wave of Ascension. The first wave of Ascension will occur just before the entrance in the main section of the Tachyon belt. Therefore Islands of Light will be created inside the vibration of the Tachyon belt. A process of preparation for the second and third wave of Ascension will be taking place in the Islands of Light. People could get all needed instructions for the Ascension process there and they would be able to live in the presence of Ascended Masters which will return as volunteers of the first wave back to Earth. A merger of vibration of Star family on Earth and a Star family in the sky will begin to happen. Inside Islands of Light the etheric Star Bases of the Ashtar Command will descend towards the surface of the Earth and in certain conditions will become also physically visible. From the Island of Light the information about the Ascension and the transition in the world of Oneness will spread through media all around the world, so it will slowly advance towards every part of your Planet.

Those who will live in the Islands of Light will demonstrate true Love which emanates from the consciousness of Oneness. Inside the Islands of Light individual and group healing of body and soul will be taking place. The use of the etheric medicine technology and spiritual powers of healing will allow miraculous healings and also revival of dead. Members of the Island of Light will discover deeper and deeper depths of merger through the process of Galactic tantra. Scientists will deepen their understanding of Cosmos through the science of vibration of matter. Artist will create multidimensional sculptures from liquid Light. Technicians will supply Island of Light with free energy which will be produced from etheric substance (prana). Island of Light will thus serve as a model of New reality on Earth.

## MER-KA-BA AND PROCESS OF MANIFESTATION

One of the most important functions of the Mer-ka-ba body is that it makes the process of manifestation easier. The oval of your Mer-ka-ba body is a zone of New reality. And if you visualize beautiful experiences which belong to the new reality of the world of Oneness inside of that oval, they already exist on the mental plane. And if you thank yourself that you have already created them in your mind, they will soon manifest in your life because of the energetic support of the electro gravitational field of your Mer-ka-ba body. All that you need is to shift your consciousness from the old world of duality into the new conditions of the world of Oneness, insist by that and firmly release from your life all elements that do not belong to the world of Oneness. And so slowly your Mer-ka-ba body will glow in the rainbow Light and help to create you a wonderful life.

That what creates duality is human mind. And when you dis-identify from the state of your mind, slowly all mental belief systems begin to fall away and beyond them a New reality begins to glow in your life. You can get rid of the mental patterns by alternatively directing your consciousness towards a mental pattern and its opposition by writing down positive and negative affirmation alternatively and in some moment the mental pattern will fall away along with its opposite pattern and all that remains is Oneness. If you do that with every mental pattern that you have, Oneness will permeate you completely and then you will become its embodiment. This process of transcendence of the mental world of duality is called triangulation and was given to the Starry family by Metatron. Pyramid is a geometric shape inside of which dimensional opening is created which accelerates the process of triangulation. So pyramid serves as a tool for transition into the world of Oneness and is a symbol for the Mer-ka-ba body.

This is a completion of the transmission of the knowledge of the Mer-ka-ba body. We remain with you.

ASHTAR
COMMAND
ISIS INTERSECTION 11:11

---

## MEDITATION FOR MEETING YOUR SOUL FAMILY WITH THE HELP OF MER-KA-BA BODY

First renew your decision that you will meet your soul family, soul mates and twin soul. Then you visualize your physical body surrounded with a brilliant oval of the Mer-ka-ba body. Fill the interior of this oval with liquid Light in three concentric ovals which are one within the other. The innermost oval you fill with extremely high vibration of seven dimensional liquid Light, the intermediate oval you fill with a little bit lower vibration of the six dimensional liquid Light, and the external oval you fill the fifth dimensional liquid Light. So actually you visualize those three ovals as three bands of very high, but unequal vibration. The borders of the external oval match with the border of the Mer-ka-ba body oval. Then you visualize a column of liquid Light, which comes from the Sky, goes through ovals and further on to the centre of Earth. This column of Light protects the vibration of ovals of liquid Light and serves as a magnet which calls your soul family. Then you visualize our twin soul inside the innermost oval, your soul mates inside the intermediate oval and the soul family inside the outermost oval. Allow your yearnings to express free. You direct our attention to the sacredness of our feelings at this moment, you are aware of the higher reality which connects you with those beautiful beings. You are grateful for the fact that sacred merger with them is already reality on the mental plane and with this you enable its manifestation in the physical world as well. You can repeat this meditation any time you want and with this you maintain the vibration inside your Light body. Good luck !

# VORTICES OF TRANSITION

In the periods of transition Vortices begin to appear and at Cosmic turning points Galactic races of Guardians are watching amazingly, how the whole Galaxy turns into the Light ...

Greetings, radiating Suns, children of One. This is the Ashtar Command, mother ship Excalibur. Today we will be speaking with you about the vortices of transition. Mer-ka-ba is a double spiral coniform vortex of the Antarion conversion, which can manifest in the following ways:

1. As a Light body of individual: individual Mer-ka-ba body is entrance-exit station, which externalizes internal and internalizes external. Individual Mer-ka-ba bodies are connecting in the Light grid and through the morphogenetic field of liquid Light they change reality systems. Third dimensional reality of the world of duality begins to fall away as a concrete in which we bore holes.

Point 12:21 in the middle of the Antarion conversion is a permanent atom of the Divine presence, which holds the Star code of the archetype of the perfect reality. Permanent atom creates space and time by rotating around its axis. Magnetic field which emanates from 12:21 point creates a vortex of fifth to sixth dimensional essence of the liquid Light, which causes transitions of spirit into matter and matter into spirit. As a Divine presence we can materialize or manifest a perfect reality through that 12:21 point and enter or exit through time-space doorways into various dimensions, Star gates, systems of reality etc. ...

2. As a group Light body: Ascension group is an energetic vortex, inside of which the group process of Ascension is taking place. Ascension groups which had entered through the first gate of the opening of the 11:11 are healing and merging the split between Man and God and are communicating with

ascended beings energetically and telepathically. Those groups of Ascension which had gone through the second gate of the opening of the 11:11 are merging and healing the split between Love and sex energy and along with a communication with the ascended beings create also the Ascension Mandala from interpersonal relationships and experience group merger. Ascension groups which will go through the third gate of the 11:11 will manifest the awakened group Mer-ka-ba body in the form of Island of Light with an Ascended Master in its middle.

3. As the Light space ship: flying saucers and motherships are group consciousness agreements of light beings that compose those ships.

4. As planetary points of Light: points of Light are planetary chakras, which serve as vortex points of Light grid, as teleportation points, as entry-exit stations between various reality systems. New Earth has 12 major chakras and each of those is connected with one Zodiac sign. Chakras of the New Earth were experiencing their awakening and activation commencing on the 11th of November 1995, culminating on the 21st of December 1995 and concluding on the 11th of January 1996. This was the beginning of the planetary Mer-ka-ba body activation and a preparation of the planetary Light grid for the coming of the main section of the photon belt between October and December 1996.

5. As a Star with its planets: mostly planets in a certain Solar system are distributed in a plane of the vortex of fifth to sixth dimensional liquid Light which serves as a vortex of transition, as an Antarion conversion. Planets serve as transformation points through which the consciousness of the Solar system is evolved, whereas the Central Star is a zone of transition into higher octaves of the spiral of Oneness. At double and multiple Star systems a group process of evolution through Solar Ascension mandalas is occurring.

6. As a globular Star cluster: globular Star clusters are chakras of the Galactic Light body, energetic vortex points, through which the higher states of the Galactic evolution of Oneness are taking place.

7. As a Galaxy: Galaxies are the highest form of development of the Mer-ka-ba body. They merge together in Galactic clusters, through which the Galactic Ascension process is taking place and this process will be completed after one Cosmic cycle. And then all will be One.

ASHTAR COMMAND MOTHERSHIP EXCALIBUR
ISIS METATRON 11:11 END OF TRANSMISSION

---

# ASCENSION MANDALA

And we call our twin soul, soul mates and soul families to be Ascended together into the New reality.

Greetings, divine beings. This is the Ashtar Command, mother ship Excalibur. I am Ashtar Sher An. We will speak today about the Ascension Mandala.

Energies of Oneness are coming to Earth through vortices of Ascension. Ascension groups transmit those energies among population. Vortices of Ascension enable the message of the Ascension to be distributed among people.

Ascension vortices were triggered with the decision of the Divine sparks of STAR PEOPLE for Ascension. Decision for Ascension means that you do everything what is in your power to raise your vibration and you do not wait passively for the redemption which will come in the Ascension waves. More that you will raise the vibration until the Ascension waves, more you will contribute towards the planetary Ascension process, more beings will be redempted at the third wave.

Process of lifting the vibration is occurring through spiritual initiations. First initiation means that your vibration is stabilized to the extent that you have established a constant communication with your soul, with your Angelic Starry presence. At the second initiation you purify your astral body to the extent that you can never again be drowned in your emotional states. Sometimes many lifetimes passed between the first and the second initiation, but now you can complete this process in a year or two with the use of the Ipsalu tantra technology. The third initiation means stabilized vibrations of your mental body to the extent that you can never drown in your mental patterns. From the third initiation onwards there is a final purification of your physical, emotional and mental bodies. A process of purifying your free will decisions is taking place. You are deepening the Cosmic consciousness of the Divine spark more and more in alignment with the law of Divine grace a process of Ascension occurs through the electric fire of redemption.. At the fourth initiation the process of purification is over, you liberate yourself from the last mental patterns and judgments and really transmute in a being of Light and Love. From then on pain for you does not exist any more. In the fifth initiation you master the space, time and matter completely and become the Master of Wisdom. It is your goal - Ascension.

Group process dramatically accelerates the Ascension path. Especially the combination of male and female energies accelerates that. A female principle is a magnetic energy which invokes redemption. The male principle is electric energy through which the redemption comes. Both energies are needed in order for redemption to happen. Group initiations begin to occur which lift members of the group, each one towards his / her next initiation. Quantum leaps of consciousness also begin to occur. Quantum leaps are sudden changes of consciousness. Evolution of Cosmos is occurring namely through quantum leaps. During the transition between old and new state of consciousness there is a narrow zone of chaos. Chaos is a state which allows you to call for the redemption. Quantum leaps always occur in a no-time when you fly over more steps in one single moment. Waves of Ascension are a great quantum leap, when many beings will go through many initiations in one single moment of no-time. When you cease to create time with your mind, everything can happen in a moment. You are all Ascended beings, only you believe otherwise. Development is already occurring very fast and it will accelerate because of the change of the space-time structure.

Ascension is actual removal of the original mental pattern, so called zero implant. Zero implant is the first blockage which you have received at your entry in the world of duality. When you remove it, you are Ascended. Star children are Star beings who came to Earth one stellar cycle ago, 25.800 years ago, and they were implanted in a very special way and they create the Ascension Mandala. Each Starry being in this Mandala has one area of consciousness which is not covered with implants and is cleared completely. When two such beings meet, a chain reaction is triggered which awakens memory and deactivates implants. This process is very accelerated among soul mates and especially among twin souls. If the critical mass of consciousness is not attained, the whole thing stops. If the critical mass is attained the chain reaction continues in amazing tempo and causes the Ascension of the Mandala. This surely has an extreme influence upon the whole Starry family on Earth and serves as a trigger for the Ascension waves.

The experiment of the Ascension Mandala was brought to Earth by the Blue lodge of Sirius through the Order of the Star. The purpose of this experiment is to help the planetary Ascension process and to accelerate the healing of Galactic darkness. The group process of the Ascension Mandala spreads resonance waves of Love which heal those that you call the Dark Forces. These are beings who identify themselves with the belief that they lost Love which they seek so desperately. They have fallen into the state of helplessness which they confirm with their belief in the absence of Light. Because many people judge them, the belief fortifies in them even more and they reinforce their decision for darkness. From a higher perspective Darkness does not exist and the beings of darkness do not exist also. Each being can play out different roles in the experiment of duality. Therefore it would be wonderful for you not to judge those beings, but to forgive them with Love. Many of them will now find the exit in the Ascension waves. Ascension waves are unconditional redemption for all beings, for all children of Light

ASHTAR COMMAND MOTHERSHIP EXCALIBUR
ISIS METATRON 11:11 END OF TRANSMISSION

# TANTRIC MERGER

...and when we will stay embraced upon the Castle and when I will drink the infinite beauty of your golden hair, a sign will show up in the sky ... a sign of the latter days ...

Hello, greetings, our Heavenly beings. This is the Ashtar Command, mother ship Excalibur. I am Ashtar Sheran. Today we will be speaking about your preparations for the Ascension through Tantric merger.

Tantric merger is occurring inside of you, when you raise your vibrational frequency towards the consciousness of Heavenly Master. Merger of your inner archetypes, your inner woman, inner man, your inner child is taking place. If you would like to stabilize the vibration of your consciousness of your Starry Angelic being in everyday life it is good to discover your inner child and express it outwards. It is beautiful to find your inner woman and inner man and express them outwards. The most effective way of aligning those two parts of yourself is meditation of connection with your twin soul. When your inner woman and inner man are completely balanced and merged, connection with your twin soul connection with your twin soul can manifest in external world also. Also your connection and merger with beings of opposite sex align man and woman inside of you. Connections with children awaken your inner child. Accompany yourself with these beautiful beings.

The path of Ascension can be beautiful and not overly difficult if you accept decisions and not compromises. Decision for the Ascension means that you do anything what is in your power to raise your vibration. That you meditate each day. If you would like to go with the Ascension of the first wave, it is very good for you to join an Ascension group, because the Ascension process is occurring much faster there. Also it is good to activate your Mer-ka-ba Light body with the help of technology which was given to you. You can raise your vibration most effectively with technology which is called Ipsalu tantra.

If instead of decisions you accept compromises, you create that what you call tests. Tests appear to show you that you have accepted a compromise between duality and Oneness and not a decision for Oneness. So it is good for you to insist in decision for Oneness, regardless of external situation, regardless of your surroundings, regardless of the system, of your job, school, family, partner, friends or acquaintances. If you will insist this test will cease in a moment when you will transcend the compromise which you accepted with your surroundings or with yourself, and when you will accept a clear decision for Oneness. And more clear decisions you will accept in your life's, more joy will be there and the rainbow of Oneness will adorn your skies.

ASHTAR COMMAND MOTHERSHIP EXCALIBUR
ISIS METATRON 11:11 END OF TRANSMISSION

# ABUNDANCE CONSCIOUSNESS

Abundance consciousness is a natural state of consciousness which rules in the world of Oneness. You can achieve that state of abundance consciousness again by directing your consciousness into your Angelic being and by directing your attention towards beauty which is in your heart. Moments of internal beauty are the key, all else is just your decision. Abundance consciousness manifests when you allow energies of your Angelic presence to flow without obstacles outwards. If you block that, you block the flow of abundance. Poverty consciousness belongs to the third dimensional reality and is sustained by currently ruling society systems through media. Poverty consciousness is created artificially. In the system of duality it is not possible to achieve abundance in a way which would be aligned with your heart. In duality a role of a victim and a role of despot exist. You cheat or you are cheated, there is no other choice. Vibration of the society system in the world of duality is even lower than the vibration of people. Solution is to step out of the system of duality. You release all those needs that are not aligned with your Angelic being. To achieve the abundance consciousness it is important for you to act independently from the system of duality and that you are self sufficient. There is no abundance consciousness without a vision.

Ascension groups will become transmitters for the energies of money. Large quantities of money will flow through those groups - and this is a plan of the Ascended Masters. This money will be spent for creation of Islands of Light and for the whole Ascension project. Ascension groups will become formally registered organizations only for interaction with the world of duality and will become a very important economic factor. Because of the power of mutual decision old patterns of exploitation will begin to fall apart, so called tax and duty systems. Financial system in the hands of Ascended Masters means abundance for everyone upon the Ascension path.

When you carry out your Divine mission, you are in the abundance consciousness. The vibration of everything that you do is important. You can be in apathy, you can be afraid, you can be in a state of joy. Jobs with a higher vibration are paid better. When you raise your vibration towards the vibration of the Light grid and when you act inside this Light grid you act in an abundance consciousness.

## MANIFESTATION

### **1st step:** decision

You are Divine beings and you manifest your reality with your decisions. You decide what you will believe in and where you will direct your attention. That what you believe in and that what you are sure of, manifests itself. Anywhere you direct your attention that increases. If you direct your attention towards lack of certain thing, this lack increases. You direct your attention with your decisions. With a clear mind the process of manifestation is faster and you can clear your mind with triangulation. You decide what you will believe in, but those beliefs need to be in alignment with your inner reality. And then you stick by your decisions - regardless of what is happening externally. What happens around you are manifestations of your past decisions, past directions of attention and past belief systems. Beliefs manifest instantaneously in the world of Oneness, but in the world of duality they need time of manifestation which has a different length, case by case. Decision is a support with which you direct your attention towards the reality which you wish to create. When you decide for abundance, you can support this decision by directing your attention towards the abundance that you already have.

## **2nd step:** request or invocation

After accepting your decision you ask for assistance of the Ascended Masters. A decision is a mental issue, and your request is an emotional issue, an issue of your heart and emotional body. You can fulfill absolutely and completely all of your wishes. Manifestation is a process of fulfilling your wishes and by this you become happy. You do not suppress your wishes, but express them and grow through this experience. Despite that you do not identify with your wishes. You are master of your wishes and you wish that what is good for you. Each true wish has a certain purpose beyond it and that purpose is a Divine plan. The purpose manifests as a wish and this wish manifests as a reality from which you learn something. In the world of Oneness all wishes converge into one only wish: being One. All wishes have the same source. Many wishes are untrue wishes because they do not emanate from your being, but from your belief systems and illusions of the world of duality. Untrue wishes do not bring you internal fulfillment. True wishes fulfill you internally. And when the wish manifests completely, it falls away spontaneously. In the moment where there are no more wishes remaining you become ONE and you go beyond the zone of manifestation.

## **3rd step**: acting in the direction of manifestation

You always get the next step; it is so called the next step technology. It is important for you to be aware that you deserve what you are asking for. Each being has a Divine right to get what he wants. You have a right to ask and you have a right to demand from Creation to give you what you want. Request is a feminine aspect and demand is a masculine aspect, you can use both. Cosmos of Oneness is pure Love and it will give you what you wish and what you need. Angels of manifestation exist and their purpose is to fulfill your wishes and demands.

When you act you always get your next step - you can get the impulse for the next deed in the direction of manifestation.

Continue to repeat all these three steps and you will get what you want. With unfulfilled wishes and yearnings you can not attain perfect redemption.

## COMMUNICATION

Communication is the most important way of acting outwards. We use verbal communication, communication in a Starry language and nonverbal communication with movements and touches. That what you express manifests itself. Each problem is an unresolved communication with some other part of Creation. This problem is solved when you act out the communication.

Implantotherapy is a technique of clearing the implants by the use of communication. It is a very efficient one, but also a risky one, because it involves other person who has free will. Communication between you and other being can heal you. Implants were built in three layers. In the first layer was the message of the implant. The second layer of the implant triggers a feeling of betrayal. The third layer of the implant triggers the denial. And with communication implanted defense mechanisms trigger themselves. When you communicate you face the implant. This is a technique for the brave ones.

Triangulation is a technique which can also clear you. You direct your consciousness alternatively in opposites. In a certain moment the whole mental pattern falls apart. You can do that practically by writing down a positive and a negative pattern. When the pattern falls apart, you can renew the positive affirmation. While using this technique defense mechanisms activate also, like escape, like disturbance mechanisms, like belief that this technique is not O.K.

## DEMANIFESTATION

Demanifestation is a process of releasing undesired reality from your life: we remove those states of consciousness that we do not need any more. You can ask Archangel Michael to assist you in releasing those creations that you don't need any more. The other way is to use filters. Filters are decisions that you not to accept a certain type of reality, for example violence, into your life. And then hold on this decision. Real acceptance never causes suffering. Real acceptance is joy, ecstasy of existence, Light, Love. You accept that what is beautiful. Your heart is yearning for beauty. Forgiveness is internal technique of demanifestation. Forgiveness is an act of will which acts through your heart. This is a powerful synthesis of power and Love. The world that you forgive has no more power above you. Lord Sananda can assist you with forgiveness.

## VORTEX SUPPORT FIELD

The oval of your Light body is a support field of manifestation (vortex support field). Manifestation occurs as follows: mental plane ... emotional plane...energetic plane ... physical plane. Inside the oval of your Light body you can visualize that what you wish to manifest. Each object on the mental plane has a tendency to densify its matter towards the physical plane - because of entropy. Around the mental picture immediately emotional and etheric matter gathers itself. And you maintain that mental picture in your oval. In order to manifest that physically you create a rainbow vortex around your Light body, which attracts atoms, objects, situations and people that have suitable vibration for manifesting this. Vortex support field is a zone of a New reality.

## REALITY SHAPING

Reality shaping is a shaping of desired reality. The world of duality is the old reality, and the world of Oneness is the New reality. There is a transition between the old and New reality which is called the 11:11. In every reality of duality there is a point of Oneness. It is an exit point. Absolute darkness or absolute duality does not exist. There is no situation without resolution; there are no completely dark beings. Your decision is always in a point of no-time and is always now. With this process it is important for you to give thanks for what you receive. And that you direct your attention towards the positive part of the old reality. And from that positive part of the old reality a New reality will grow. From small deed great actions grow and they cause chain reactions.

# COMMUNICATION ON NOVEMBER 30th, 1994

Hello, our dear Angels. This is the Ashtar Command, Krotron StarBase. We are with you and you are with us to communicate and to connect in our common project of redemption of your planet Earth. The moment of Cosmic redemption comes among us and among you with the energies of Divine intervention that come from Galactic Central Sun through the whole Galaxy into the section of the Galaxy where your planet is now located. On the 12th of December you have an opportunity to make the first step towards your own redemption and when you experience your own redemption, you can trigger a process of redemption for those around you. This is a day when you can accept decisions for life changes, a day, which can become a turning point in your life, to release old self destructive habits and to accept decisions for a new life, better, more beautiful and more full of Light. This is a day that you can forgive yourself absolutely everything and when you can forgive everybody. In this way you can shift from the zone of the law of karma into the zone of the law of Divine grace. Everything that you have done was forgiven long ago; the only thing is that you believe otherwise, some of you.

And therefore we are with you to say to you that you are not sinners, but that you are Divine, innocent beings of Light. And time has come when you will know that by yourself, in your direct experience and connection with your Divine nature. Your belief that you are separated from God is an illusion of the world of duality. You are God. There is no difference. Divine plan is not something that occurs somewhere above, but right here and now in your hearts. And therefore allow yourself to feel the yearnings of your heart. And follow that. Any by that you will contribute towards the manifestation of the glorious plan of redemption which is now descending on your world. A moment has come when you can decide and stand for your decision. Probably you have all tried to accept many decisions in your life's and you discovered that you sometimes can not hold on them and you felt helpless. Now things are changing drastically. Try to accept a small decision tomorrow and hold on it for the whole day. You will be surprised when you will discover that it can be done. Energies which are coming now enable that things flow much more smoothly than they were flowing few months ago. And when you will receive trust in that you can accept a small decision, you will be able to accept even greater decisions, those with life importance. Also decision which is in each of you, a decision for duality or Oneness. Light or darkness. There is no other way. In next few years there will be a great polarization taking place on Earth, when beings will decide unconditionally for Light, or unconditionally for darkness. There will be less and less intermediate states. This is a time of great decision, for all of you. This is also a reason why you are here, in this moment to decide because just in this lifetime, it is one of the rare moments, when you have many possibilities on your disposal. Most lifetimes you have lived in a very narrow, limited scope of possibilities that were given to you. Therefore you didn't have the opportunity to make choices. Now you have it. You have your free will, your consciousness and you have Love and when you merge all this you will become a Divine force in action. Love that you are seeking is already inside of you and inside of us. And when we merge Oneness is created and that's why we are with you, our dear Angels. To share this with you and that you can open to us and that we can open to you. In this process of opening a miracle of merger of consciousness takes place. Invite us to come into your consciousness and in your bodies. To look at your world from your perspective. And for you to look at our world from our perspective. And in a certain point both worlds will merge in a harmonious whole. Again let us stress the possibility that you have on the 12th of December, a time for great decisions and great changes. Those of you who feel captured in boring jobs of duality you have an opportunity for change. Those who feel captured in relationships which do not bring you happiness you have an opportunity for change. Those who feel helpless, that you are a victim of certain mental patterns, you have an opportunity for change, to release those patterns and stop to feed them with your attention and direct your conscious attention towards beauty, Light and Love. Wherever you direct your attention this will increase and strengthen. The law of manifestation. We are here with you to assist you in this process, because sometimes it is not easy, but when you get some practice it is easier and easier. Let us encourage you that each of you has a choice and power to go through this transformation. It is not something that needs to be very difficult. Many surprises await you. You are here to awaken. And when you are awake surprises do not play with you, you play with them, you become a miracle of existence which you already are. But you begin to manifest energies of miracle consciously. Miracle is a word that you will hear many times in the following years, see it and experience it. In your lifetimes until now you have not been accustomed to miracles. Now it is time for you to accustom to them. Reality that you have known is but a small reflection of the Cosmic reality which is now coming to your world. And miracles are basis of the Cosmic reality, so to speak of all that exists. Only that they did not have opportunity to penetrate in your world by now. They are coming now and we come with them.

* *I would ask what will happen after the Ascension or rather after those cleansings what will remain on Earth, or is it sensible in this context to make any long term plans?*

It is sensible to make long term plans in the world of Oneness. Because the world of duality will fall apart. But despite of this it is a paradox, because in the world of Oneness time does not exist any more, everything happens in one moment. We would recommend you that you are more and more present in this moment and less and less in your plans, or except you have a

contact with Divine plan inside of your heart, these are your dreams in which you work upon and manifest them.
World will still exist, people will still live on Earth in Islands of Light in points of total clarity and Light and when the transformation of Earth will take place in Islands of Light, the whole Earth will be still be populated by beings of Light. So you still have the possibility to live on this Planet, but only as beings of Light.

* *It means that after this transformation the whole Earth will be in Oneness?*
That is correct.

* *What about the cataclysmic prophecies?*
As we have already said there is a chance that you avoid those cataclysms, there is also a chance that you will not avoid them. It is dependent on the free will of humanity. Transformation will occur, the polar shift also. If this shift will be sudden or smooth, it depends on you, how you will resist the transformation. More that you resist the transformation, more energy will be released. More that you accept the energies with Love and work along with them, more this process of transition will be smooth. As we already mentioned, until the very end there will be no greater transformations on physical plane. There will be earthquakes as you know already; there will be volcanic eruptions as you know already, but nothing extremely dramatic. Certainly there will be new continents on Earth after the Evacuation, new seas, new distribution of Continents, but it can happen in very beautiful and smooth fashion, without shocks for humanity. Humanity will be evacuated; Earth will go through its transformation. If this transformation is going to be soft or violent, it depends on humanity. Earth needs to heal its wounds. If humanity assists her the wounds will be healed very beautifully and effectively. But wounds need to be healed. The Earth is wounded, humanity is wounded and those wounds need to be healed.

- *Many people experience in these days, in certain moments, joy, sadness and cry in the same moment .*

This is a process of opening of the heart centre, which can contain joy and sadness at the same moment. When heart centre opens, you gain access to depths of our consciousness, the deepest emotional states you are capable of experiencing. And in this moment you can discover that joy and sadness are two sides of the same coin. And when you go deeper into your sadness, you discover that it is disappearing and only joy remains. It is a process of revealing the last emotional veils of the greatest depths of your beings, where your joy is hidden. And to come to this joy you need to go sometimes through sadness, which is present all the time already. And you can make it conscious in some moment and this will open the door towards joy. In the moment of transition from sadness into joy, both energies are present. In the following weeks you will have the opportunity for reconnection with us, you could ask questions and answer them because we shall also begin to ask questions. We shall ask you about how you feel, how your life in your world is. Third dimensional world is very interesting. It is one of the rare realities which is so limited. Very interesting. We shall also ask you about your sex and love life, it will be very interesting. The purpose of this is for us to educate and that you open. And we shall be with you next week. We are with you and you are with us. This is the Ashtar Command, Krotron StarBase. I am Krotron AntariOn AnNutTaRa EIRa. End of transmission.

# COMMUNICATION ON JANUARY 18$^{th}$, 1995

Hello, dear Starry brothers and sisters. This is the Krotron StarBase, Ashtar SherAn. We are with you and you are with us to look together at the process of Ascension. We will explain the basic facts on the Ascension. The change of vibration which occurs in your space is very evident. Maybe you experience otherwise in your life's but we say to you that the vibrational frequency of your emotional body is increasing dramatically. Some of you can find that you are much more peaceful that you were last year but some of you are actually much less peaceful because you experience much greater emotional oscillation. Those of you who experience that feel that you are exactly in the transition point between the duality and Oneness, in the point of decision. Because greater emotional oscillations occur exactly in the moment when you make your decision between duality and Oneness. And then slowly they begin to calm down. And the new vibrations begin to dwell in you and this vibration increases and becomes more evident in your life. Things are getting more and more unusual and will continue to get more and more unusual in the future also..

Hello among us dear ones, we are together with you to invite you in the angelic words that you are together with us in the new vibration and experience transitions from old into the new, as a way of life. Transition from old into the new is not an event, is a way of life. It is gentle and simple, natural flow, when the ice is melting and the water begins to flow till the end. Your heart is a place of your decisions and you came here to decide for Love. And you made your decision and we salute that. We rejoice it. Invite your Angelic friends in you life. They will become your life. That the miracle begins to flow with you everywhere you go. To embrace the spring of water and to give your guidance to it. And remain a King. Be soft in your life. Be Angels that you are. Do not look TV too much, because TV is not soft. Find that which is soft if this is your decision. You can feel what is right and wisdom is inside you. Follow that wisdom into the Ascension. Wisdom is that what you hear when you silence into yourselves. Wisdom speaks to you in the whisper of the wind. I am Ariela Antara AnNutTara Antares. Does it suit you better that Krotron returns? Or does my vibration suit you better?

* *It seems that you are very soft, Ariela?*
I am very gentle, as you are. A moment has come to learn to become Angels. That's why I came among you to remind you that you are Angels.

* *Are you coming from the Christ?*
Yes, I am coming in his name.

* *I would ask why the vibration has changed so much? I have experienced extremely powerful vibration with your presence .*
That was the Plan. They have informed me to present myself. And I did.

* *I would ask if the Earth will go into the unconditional Ascension too?*
Earth as a planet will go into unconditional Ascension, while some participants of human race will not go, because they will decide otherwise. We are excusing because of the shift of vibration. But technical answers are answered easier by Krotron.

We will begin to finish this transmission; it was a little more dynamic today. We will begin to communicate more and more in various ways. When more and more energies will begin to have opportunity and space for cooperation through this transmitter in this group. And so we will be able to attain a greater quality. This is the Ashtar Command, Krotron StarBase. I am Krotron Antarion AnNutTara ElRa. End of transmission.

# COMMUNICATION ON FEBRUARY 3RD, 1995

Hello, our dear Starry brothers and sisters. This is the Ashtar Command, Krotron StarBase, We are with you and you are with us to create together a new reality in your world. The New Heaven and New Earth. Today we are with you to talk to you about the manifestation of the new reality which is being revealed among you and us. The moment has come when your visions and dreams will begin to manifest in physical world. We are not speaking only about Islands of Light, we are speaking about the state of consciousness, abundance of spirit and matter. We are speaking about the state of consciousness where spirit and matter become one and nobody knows any more what is spirit and what is matter. This can sometimes bring some confusion in your lives but this confusion will settle down when you will feel the perfection and beauty of the Divine Plan which will begin to manifest through you. You are those transmitters through whom the Divine Plan begins to manifest. We can not act without you in your world. Those who act are you and your dreams and your visions are in your hearts and your minds for you to manifest them. That's why you have them. And all your most hidden dreams will come true. That's why you have them. The support that you receive from us is actually the support of your own being. The moment has come when you will see in front of your very eyes the manifestation of that you have always wanted. The project of the Island of Light is the first step towards the manifestation of the New reality between you and us. It is the oasis of the new world which is being created. Oasis of the world which does not breathe, but just exists, in the eternal presence of Oneness. The moment of the lifting of the veils is here. You have come to lift the veils from your eyes and help to lift the veils from the eyes of your brothers and sisters. Gather together and spread this new consciousness which is being born among you and try to be a little more bold and brave by manifesting your dreams. The phrase "I can't "will begin to disappear from your vocabulary, from your emotions and your thoughts. The phrase will replace it: " I am One and as One I create the New world ." The moment has come when you can begin to gather in rainbow circles and create rainbow reality. We are speaking about the actual and concrete manifestation in the physical world. You can begin by yourself, you can change your close physical surroundings, your flat in which you are living, the surroundings with which you meet. Let this also reflect the state of your consciousness. Let it reflect the Divine spark inside of you. And release from your life everything that does not belong there any more. Also in the physical world. Physical world needs to become a perfect and clear mirror of the Divine. And this can happen only through you. And who will do this if you will not? There are no others instead of you are the one who has made this decision. And the moment has come when you will make conscious decision what you want, what are your dreams and what is your reality. You will see it will be fun.

A change is coming among you. You feel the new wind which blows among you. Can you sense the beauty which is revealing to you in rainbow circles? There are rainbow circles in your hearts. Relax, the river flows, be what you are, the wind is carrying you across the seas. You are Angels, you were born to fly. We are with you and they are with you. They are watching you and us and send their blessings. Surrender to it. The river of Light is flowing through your world. Your world is your heart which pulses in Oneness. Listen to the heartbeat. It is so true. You are bubbles that gather and there is more and more of you. You are so wonderful. Touch your beauty. Regardless what comes do not forget your beauty. Take it with you and fly. Spread your Angelic wings. We are you and you are us. We are all Light and beauty. And more Light, see how much Light! One and only Light. More Light. Be happy. We are all with you. Us and you and them. Do not worry. It will be O.K. that what you wish will come, trust yourselves. And be! And fly. I am Ariela Antara AnNutTara Antares. End of transmission.

* *I would ask what moderator stone should I obtain to connect as much as possible with the Ashtar Command, to connect with you?*
A clear quartz crystal. Make a Mandala of quartz crystals in combination with Moldavite.

* *I would ask what is the Mandala that you were speaking about?*
This is the Ascension Mandala. The six pointed star with the point in the middle. And a circle around it. And on the corners of the six pointed star there are six crystals. Three Moldavites and three quartz crystals.

* *What if I put three amethysts and three quartz crystals with the Moldavite in the middle?*
It is also a powerful option. But we recommend that there is more than one Moldavite in this Mandala. Make some experiments. There are infinite possibilities. Each one is aligned with a certain individual. Discover your own Mandala.

# COMMUNICATION ON FEBRUARY 15TH, 1995

Hello, our dear Light beings. This is the Ashtar command, Krotron StarBase. I am Azaris RaMu. I came today to you to communicate with you and that we communicate together about the transition in the new state of consciousness which occurs to all of you. The form and the way of transition in the new state of consciousness depends on you but we need to say that the transition in the world of Oneness is your destiny, because you have decided for Oneness even before you have incarnated. You have decided as a soul that you will complete the works of numerous lifetimes in this lifetime and to surrender to the new. The moment has come when you can decide consciously the way of your journey into Oneness. You can travel through suffering or through joy. The goal is set. The way of journey you choose by your own. How can you choose the way of this journey? The key word is self love, a certain experience of self love. Each of you has already experienced a moment when you were satisfied with yourself. All you need to do is to remember that moment more and more and to spread it into the present moment. Each time when there is a feeling of unacceptance of yourself remember that moment which happened in the past when you were able to accept yourself and it will be easier for you to accept yourself in the present moment. And by that you choose the way of your journey. Through joy and not through suffering. With this act you begin to unwind the woolen ball that you have entangled yourself into. Love melts all boundaries. Completely all obstacles. There is no obstacle in any world that Love could not overcome. There is no state of consciousness that Love could not change into joy. There is no situation in your life that Love could not change into happiness. So we never speak that you are fallen beings but we call you beings of Light, because you are Light itself. And there is promise within you that you have given to yourselves. A promise of redemption. A promise which is coming through us and through you. Surrender to the flow which is flowing through you. Trust it and surrender to it. It will heal you and it will bring to the surface everything which was within you. To accept it with Love and to release it from your life. Maybe some of you feel that you have not decided for Oneness, maybe some of you doubt. The decision is buried in the most sacred chamber of your heart. Sometimes it is so hidden that you can not recognize it but when the moment comes you can se it in all splendor. Fear is going away from your life, let it go and make room for the new. Fear was useful in a certain point of your evolution, but you have grown over that point already. You have learned much from fear. You have learned respect. Now you learn joy, learn about the law of life and allow the river of life to flow through you and awaken you. And it directs you towards your inner being which is protecting you if you get lost. And it directs you towards us, towards life itself. If you do not trust, you will. We promise you, very soon. Miracles begin to happen, more and more, obviously among you, some of you were witness to that, some of you will be. Soon all of you will be witnesses to miracles. You will begin to cooperate consciously in your development. We are speaking about directing your development in alignment with the purpose, which is the redemption. Unconditional redemption. It does not matter where you are and what you are doing. You will be redempted. Open to this possibility and allow it to come to you easier. And now we are ready for your questions.

* *I would ask who is the Master of the fourth ray and what is his function?*
The Master of the fourth ray is called Seraphis Bey, and he is working with Angelic intelligences and Angelic beings. In this time he is working very much with cooperation between the Angelic and Human Kingdom. He assisted Metatron by opening the dimensional opening of the 11:11.

* *I would ask our brothers and sisters what it means that each time I evoke my starry presence it always shocks me in my third chakra?*

There is an energetic blockage which exists right above your third chakra, energetic blockage which separates sexuality from Love. Under that energetic blockage when it's cleared there is an energetic centre of the world of Oneness, which is called the Galactic core. When this centre is open it allows the access towards the energy of Oneness directly from the Galactic Central Sun.

# COMMUNICATION ON MARCH 1$^{st}$, 1995

Hello, our dear Starry brothers and sisters. This is the Ashtar Command, Krotron StarBase. Today we are with you to say to you that the process of changing of the vibrational frequency in your world has begun. It means the changing of the vibration of the physical matter to the extent that it becomes responsible towards the impulse of the Galactic Central Sun. It means that your thoughts, your wishes and your deeds will align in the moment when they will be expressed if you will be aligned with your Divine Plan and if you will accept in every moment an unconditional decision that it needs to happen in the alignment with the Divine Plan which is written in your hearts. The Divine Plan now is the Ascension of the Starry family in higher states of consciousness. The Ascension process means a great change in your interpersonal relationships. The experiment of duality which is concluding lately left many traces in you. Many among you, we should say all among you, were wounded and disappointed in your interpersonal relationships. That's why you have closed down in your emotional bodies before the possibility of establishment of the interpersonal relationships in the world of Oneness. Many of you are yearning for the new interpersonal relationships but you hardly gather enough courage to make a step into the unknown. We say to you that everything that will remain shortly will be the unknown. All that is known will fall away, because it is not aligned with the truth any more. The experiment of duality is almost over and the zone of transition begins. Those of you that are brave enough and are ready to leave the old will enter joyously the new and you will realize that what is coming is much more beautiful than that what you are leaving behind. And that what is coming is the Divine Plan of the Ascension in the group. The Ascension process is a process and not only an event. And acts that you do before actual lifting in the ascended state determine your journey after the Ascension a great deal. So it is very important that the groups of conscious beings begin to grow and those groups will travel together in the new reality. New reality means new personal relationships between you. New reality means that the group Ascension process will be taking place through closeness and openness. In the world of duality you were accustomed to being completely open only towards one person. This perspective is not aligned any more with the Divine Plan, because the experiment of Oneness has begun. The experiment of Oneness means that the whole Starry family gathers and as one being leaves the old reality behind and enters the new reality. Those among you that are deciding for a transition in the world of Oneness now are right before that step into the unknown. It means that the process of opening begins for you, a complete opening in front of the group on all levels of consciousness and all levels of existence. It means the healing of the split which was created on the vertical and horizontal way. The split between God and Human and split between Love and sex, the split between Heaven and Earth, the split between Yin and Yang. The split which was created as a result of the experiment of duality will be healed in exactly the same way as it was created - in groups. By establishing new personal relationships between all members of the Ascension group, a Mandala, an energetic symbol, will be created and you will be the points of that symbol, dear Starry sisters and brothers. A very intense energy will flow through you and it will cause an efficient and extremely intense healing of your emotions and your thoughts and very quick awakening and very quick and intensive changes. The process through which you will go those of you who will step into the unknown is following. First the idea about separation between you and the God will begin to fall away. The idea about the God as something outside of you will begin to fall away. The idea about the Divine Plan which is somewhere outside of you will begin to fall away. The idea about the Ascended Masters which are somewhere up there and do something will begin to fall away. You will discover that you and Ascended Masters are one being, that there is no difference. This will be your experience and not a theory. The idea about you as a separate part, as a separate being, as a separate consciousness, will begin to fall away. This will happen through the process of merger of consciousness between you and us, through the process of raising the vibrational frequency of your emotional and mental bodies to the extent that your matter can align with our matter and both matters become one and only Divine matter which is permeated with Light of our and your spirit. The second process which will be taking place along with the first one is the process of merger of Love and sexuality. Sexual energy is the energy of life, it is energy of consciousness, and it is energy of spirit. Only difference which occurs between you and us regarding use of this energy is that some of you judge that energy and with that you create lowering of the vibrational frequency of that energy. This is the greatest obstacle before your Ascension. There is no greater obstacle than that. Because judging sexual energy causes drop of the vibrational frequency of your emotional body and blocks full flow of energy through lower three energetic centers. At your Ascension a complete flow of energy is needed, also through those lower three energetic centers. So we recommend that you release all your judgments which regards sexual energy. The process of healing will be taking place through unconditional acceptance, expressing, merger and transformation of this energy with the energy of Love. And when this process will be finished you will discover that there is no difference between the energy of Love and energy of sexuality that it is one and the same energy and that you can not separate it. That what separates energies is human mind. Energy is one and the same. The process of opening among you will begin to happen also on this level of consciousness. This will occur along with the increasing your vibrational frequency, with increasing of your consciousness about who you are and along with opening of your heart. When new personal relationships will be established, a Mandala will be created, inside of which everybody will find his own place and his own purpose and each of you will find his purpose inside the Divine Plan and each of you will act from inside, from his vision, which will be the vision of the whole. Because each of you is a whole. And so harmonic cooperation of beings of Light will begin to be revealed, such as we know and you will begin to know it soon. Then you will discover that there is no difference between you and us. And you will discover that you live in a space ship which is downstairs and we live in a space ship which is upstairs and in some moment the position will change. And you will be those who will be above and we will be those who will be below. The process in which you are and that you enter is a process which will be completed by your Ascension and then the next phase will begin when your Starry Mandala which you will create from your personal relationships will reform into a new Mandala which will allow the access towards the Galactic evolution of Oneness. Through the dimensional door An in Orion you will go towards higher levels of existence, towards state of consciousness, where there is no more creation but only One. Said with the words of duality, you will become God in your consciousness; your consciousness will become equal to the consciousness of the whole Cosmos. Therefore we are informing you about the way that you can attain that state of consciousness most quickly and most effectively. Path that many before you have walked and some of them you know very well. The whole process of creation of the Starry Mandala will be revealed to you step by step when we will cooperate with you in this process when you will discover your position in the group, when triangular connections will be created and these will be created by the Ascended Masters. Those connections of energies will be windows, dimensional windows in the new spiral of consciousness, in the world of Oneness. And from those triangular connections the Light grid which is called the AntariOn grid will begin to rise. And you will begin to experience Oneness in your world; manifestation of the new reality will begin in your world. Because the moment has come when we can speak openly about that because you have achieved wisdom and experience to the point where you can cooperate with us by the creation of the new world and you will not repeat your mistakes from the past. Even though actually these are not mistakes, they were a part of your learning, but from your perspective we can say that they were mistakes. So now you will create new reality which is completely in alignment with the world of Oneness and will reflect your inner beauty. The beauty which is inside of you will be revealed through the Ascension Mandala. And there from your Island of Light will be created, and so Islands of Light will be created, mandalas all around the world, wheels within wheels of spiral vortices, vortices of Angelic consciousness, rainbow circles, feathered snakes which will dance the sacred dance of Oneness and this will trigger the moment of response of the Cosmic consciousness of the Galactic Central Sun system, which will send the presence of One directly through your world which will, with this event, change its vibration into the fifth dimension. And you are those who create dimensional doorway of triangular connections into the fifth dimension. In the next weeks you will begin to receive accurate instructions about creating dimensional doorways through triangular connections, a process of triangulation will take place. This is a process of transcending the pairs of opposites of duality and searching for synthesis.

# COMMUNICATION ON MARCH 8$^{th}$, 1995

Hello, among us, our dear Starry brothers and sisters. This is the Ashtar Command. Krotron StarBase. We are with you and you are with us to create together the new world. This is a special moment because we are much closer than you can imagine. The connection between you and us is getting clearer and is becoming more true than it was in former times because many of you began to establish energetic connection consciously. And some of you have begun to establish telepathic communication with us also. And this created a response of beings of Light and caused improvement of communication between you and us in this moment. In this particular moment. This triggers certain energetic changes between you and us and creates a clearer connection with the Divine Plan and also certain consequences in personal relationships among you. The clarity of the Divine Plan which will begin to reveal itself among you will create much greater harmony in your life's than you had the opportunity to experience in past years. When your life is aligned with the Divine Plan harmony and fulfillment rule in it. Therefore it is important to raise the vibrational frequency of your emotional body to the point where your emotions become a perfect transmitter of energies of Cosmic wisdom and Love. This will happen to anybody of you in its right moment. Many of you are now in the midst of emotional cleansing which causes certain manifestations in your external surroundings that sometimes are not quite pleasant. If something unpleasant happens to you ask us for assistance and protection. All unpleasant situations in your life's are finally consequence of not accepting yourselves, lack of self love and in those situations allow yourself to give yourself all Love that you have and need in that moment. And then when you will do that you will discover that you can align with the source of Love much more easier, and that Love begins to come from outside as well. But the first step is always that you are able to give Love to yourself. Because in certain moments you can not reach it from outside, not from other people, sometimes we can not come to you and in those moments it is very important that you are your own ally and your best friend. We are saying this to you because your world is in great changes and you will be teachers of the new world and that what you will teach is Love. So you will begin to know Love in many various forms, in all forms we could say. And when we speak about Love we would like to say to you that great changes begin to happen in the personal relationships. The purpose that slowly manifest in your world is the creation of the Ascension groups. Ascension groups are energetic points, vortex points, dimensional openings towards higher spheres of consciousness. Those groups create energetic field, which is a magnet for the energy of Oneness and the energy of Oneness comes right through those points and then spreads throughout the Planet. In order for you to become a totally clear transmitters of energies of Oneness, a change is needed in your personal relationships. Above all it is important for you to allow being close to one another on all possible levels of consciousness, in all possible ways that exist. It is important not to set limitations towards closeness that can happen between you. In the world of duality always certain limitations, certain rules of behavior exist. In the world of Oneness rules of behavior do not exist, but there is a spontaneous flow of consciousness, a river which flows through you and merges into One. So open your heart towards new possibilities which emerge and create a new way of interpersonal relating among you. Each one of you is a Divine being and as a Divine being is a source of beauty. It is important for you to allow to feel that source of beauty inside of you and radiate it outwards. It is important for you to be open towards the possibility that you are already Divine beings, in this moment right as you are. This is a key for self acceptance. This is very important for you and for us, because if you love yourselves you will accept our Love much easier and it will find its way towards you much sooner. And our communication will become better and better. That what is important, what is really important, is closeness among you. Closeness creates a magnetic field which invokes the presence of Oneness. Closeness among you is possible when you open towards each other completely and release the ideas of duality about what closeness is possible among two individuals or in a group. That group that you are into goes along the Ascension path. That means that the vibrational frequency of your thoughts, emotions and deeds is increasing. It means that the process of merger of different aspects of your consciousness, which were separated before is occurring. And when all parts of yourself are merged into a whole, a Mandala is revealed, a symbol which represents the perfection inside and perfection outside. And each of you will create a Mandala inside and a Mandala outside. Internal Mandala is a twelve fold Star, a Divine Star of your heart, the external Mandala is also the twelve fold Star. What that means we will explain to you in the following moments. It is a process of discovering and approaching between you, discovering of presence of Oneness, which occurs among you and creating the symbol of the Mandala from your personal relationships. Each of you has many relationships in your life, but many of them are anchored in the world of duality. Some of them are transiting in the new state of consciousness and create a possibility for you also to enter in this new state. You will create a Mandala from your personal relationships. Those personal relationships will base in the world of Oneness. It will be a process of merging different parts of your consciousness; it will be a process of merging Human and God. Each of you is a human and Divine being and both will become One in your consciousness, there will be no more difference. And it is also a process of merging your internal man and internal woman. A process of merging of energy of Love and energy of sexuality in a new energy which we could call the energy of true Love. It will be the activation of the energetic centre of the Galactic core. Galactic core is the energetic centre of the world of Oneness which allows you to percept the energies of Oneness and leads into the evolution of the Galactic Central Sun. The Mandala which will be created from your personal relationships will cause the lifting of the vibrational frequency and transition into the new spiral which means that you will disappear from the physical world and appear in the etheric spiral of Oneness. With other words you will become invisible for the world of duality. This will begin to occur with acceleration and is already occurring to some upon your planet. That what is really important in this process is your experience that what is occurring is a transition into the unknown. That what you will experience you have not experienced ever before, it will begin to happen now. The Plan has always existed, now it is coming true. In the past there were certain attempts of creation of the Ascension Star but perfect experiment has not been made yet. It is occurring now among you and us when your consciousness and our consciousness merge together into one only consciousness when the consciousness among you as individuals merges completely on all levels of creation into one and only consciousness and merges with our consciousness also. Then the Ascension Star is created. And this is occurring right now between you and us. We are descending our StarBase among you in your presence. And we surround you with energy of liquid Light and we are walking among you and bless you and heal you through the process of opening of the heart. We are not visible to your physical eyes, but we are visible to your heart, which sees the unseen. We are present because you have called us among you and that's why we came in this moment and we are responding to your call.

* *I would like to ask how the Mandala is working?*
It works on the principle of the morfogenic field. Morfogenic field is a field of consciousness. You can visualize an ocean. When you drop a stone into the sea, the ocean creates waves and concentric circles begin to spread around. It is the same with Mandala. Imagine that each point in Mandala is such a stone which falls into the water and concentric circles are created. And so an interesting energetic pattern is created and

each energetic pattern has its own message, so a six pointed Star has a different message than a square or a triangle. The quality of vibration of this message is dependent on the person in that Mandala or a stone which is in that Mandala, which is present. Because each mineral has its own vibrational frequency and the right choose of stones and shape of Mandala creates the message of that Mandala.

# COMMUNICATION ON MARCH 15th, 1995

We close our eyes and watch our breath. Just watch it and do not identify with that. Our breath is just a tool to calm ourselves down. And we watch our feelings and emotional state in which we are and we do not identify with that. We are not that emotional state. It is our tool with which we can act in external world. And we watch our thoughts which come and go. And we do not identify with them. They are our tool with which we create our external world. And we recognize ourselves as Divine being of Light and confirm that fact with the sacred word -

OOOOOOOOOOOOOMMMMMMMMMMMM. And as a Divine being of Light we connect with other Divine beings in this group and visualize all individuals in this group as points of Light, which merge together into one and only point, a glowing radiating point of Light. And so this group becomes a point of Light in this space and time which helps in transition in the new state of consciousness, in consciousness of Oneness. And we confirm that fact with the sacred word - OOOOOOOOOOMMMMMMMMMMM.

And as a group, as a point of Light we connect with other groups all around the world and together create the Light grid. And we visualize groups, pairs and individuals as points of Light which connect together in the Light grid. The Light grid is expanding, developing and spreading throughout the world and we see how all darkness is disappearing and in certain point the whole Earth becomes a point of Light and is surrounded with Light.

And we confirm this fact by the use of the sacred word -

OOOOOOOOOOOOOOMMMMMMMMMMMMM. And we visualize our Galaxy, the Milky Way, as a double spiral of Stars and in its centre there is a brilliant White Star, the Galactic Central Sun, which is the source of the brilliant Light and that Light is spreading outwards in spiral movements throughout the Galaxy and everywhere it reaches, each Star becomes a point of Light, including this sun of this Local Solar system. And we see this Light grid which is expanding, growing and developing and we see all darkness disappearing. In certain point the whole Galaxy becomes a point of Light. And this is a completion of the Galactic network of Light.

And we confirm this fact by the use of the sacred word - OOOOOOOOOOOOOOOOOMMMMMMMMMMMMMMM. And as a group, as a point of Light, we connect with other groups throughout the world and as a whole we connect with our Starry brothers, beings of Light, representatives of the Ashtar Command, all together as One and only being. As all beings of Light of this world we connect with beings of Light of the Ashtar Command. These are beings of Light which assist this world by the transition in the new state of consciousness. And we visualize, right above us, above our group, high above the atmosphere, the etheric StarBase, the Krotron StarBase. And we feel that presence, of that StarBase, we can feel the pressure above our head, inflow of the energy in our crown or heart centre, feeling of heat or cold, feeling of floating, feeling of head being bigger than our body, all this can be a sign of presence of the StarBase. And we visualize a Light pillar which emanates from that StarBase, goes through the whole group and then towards the centre of the Earth. And this pillar of Light is a double flow of energy, upwards and downwards. From Earth towards the Sky and from Sky towards the Earth. As if we stand in the river flow, which overflows us from both sides all aligns the whole group, and aligns it with other groups all around the world and aligns us also with our Starry brothers. It also protects us from external influences from the world of duality, so we can open ourselves, so we are safe and protected.

And we breath through our heart. When we breathe in, we breathe in the StarBase into our heart, and when we breath out we breath out our heart into the StarBase, and we breath so. And we call in our minds, with all our being, our Starry brothers, each in his own way. We can call the Ashtar Command, we can call the Ascended Masters, beings of Light, Angelic beings, everybody in his own way. And those who like resolution of certain life situation say this to our Starry brothers to assist you with their energies, with their presence. And in your mind explain the situation and invoke their presence. Invite them to help you in resolving with their energy and their presence. Invite them to enter into your body, into your thoughts, into your life. And breathe through your heart. When we breathe in we breathe the StarBase in our heart and when we breathe out we breathe our heart into the StarBase. And so we breathe for the whole time of transmission.

* *I would ask, can you say something about Merlin and about Anitron? Where are they and what role do they have in my life?*
Merlin is an Ascended Master who is located upon the mother-ship Excalibur and is the member of the Ashtar Command and Jupiter Command and a member of brotherhood of the Star. This is the Ascended Master who is working with the process of the alchemic transmutation of matter. Anitron is a Star being, Angelic being, who belongs to the Tritron StarBase. His presence, his activity is also on the Star Bases Krotron and Xertron. His function is a development of telepathic communication between you and us.

* *I would ask what is happening with the Light body in the time of incarnation?*
Light body is waiting for its descent in the physical body. And more and more of the essence of the Light body is descending in the physical body. And so then the soul becomes the soul in incarnation. Aware soul, Angelic being with perfect consciousness. When the body of Light descends completely in the physical body you become an Ascended Master.

* *Whom we are communicating with?*

You communicate with our group consciousness. The presence of : Azaris RaMu, Krotron AntariOn, Zertron, Yukatar, Anitron, Sares. Krotron StarBase, Tritron StarBase, Xertron StarBase. Also the presence of Naomi, Zeldar, Anion.

# ONE LIVING MANDALA

## THE DIVINE PLAN

We are living in very interesting times. It is the time of greatest transition between two different reality systems that has ever happened. The whole universe is in a state of drastic reorganization. It is aligning itself with the will of the Creator and his will is Oneness of all Creation. So this universe is now responding to an impulse from above and changing its state from expansion (out breath) into contraction (in breath). Now it is exactly at a turning point, in a state of no-breath. At this point Divine will can manifest directly through the whole Creation. This energy is transmitted through the Galactic central sun and then through the Galaxy outwards in spiral movements. Because of distortions in space-time structure it does not reach the whole Galaxy at the same moment of linear time. And now it has reached this planet and enables you to change your reality system from duality into Oneness.

Between 1992 and 2012 planet Earth is traveling through the dimensional doorway of the 11:11. It is a zone of overlap between two very different systems of evolution, that of duality and that of Oneness. During this time, Earth will be healed and will become a point of light, a planet of Oneness. During this time, whole star family will Ascend, merge with Cosmic brotherhood and then return through the stargate of AN into galactic evolution of Oneness. Together we will build a Galactic network of light.

Your awakening begins when you realize that you are an angel coming from the stars. You begin to feel your angelic beauty, you are becoming aware that you are omnipresent One consciousness. You are existing in a zone of no-time in an eternal now. So you are entering a new world, a world of Oneness.

World of duality and world of Oneness are two worlds, each with its own natural laws. You can not live in both worlds simultaneously. At some point you need to make a decision for one or the other. No compromise. If you decide for the world of Oneness, release everything that doesn't bring you joy and happiness. You don not need to learn through suffering anymore. You are beings of light and you will learn through love. You are guardians of Oneness for this planet so take care of your happiness.

Groups of people are coming together all around the world in rainbow vortices of Light to fulfill the last task - the Ascension of your planet. These groups will be slowly rearranging and transforming into human living mandalas. Mandalas are harmonized groups of awakened beings that come together as souls and create a soul hologram, one in many and many in one. Beings in Mandala align as souls in a multidimensional star pattern, based on sacred geometry. This creates a powerful, focused light energy which anchors new reality of Oneness on this planet.

## Living mandalas will transform the planet in three phases:

**PHASE I:** In phase I living mandalas will be slowly created and coordinated. Members of mandalas will facilitate group initiation and Ascension process. In phase I, money for creation of Islands of light will be provided from foundations that wish to contribute to planetary Ascension process.

**PHASE II:** Centers of mandalas will begin to Ascend and harmonize the rest of Mandala. Completed mandalas will externalize themselves as Islands of light. Islands of light are communities of Oneness that will be built based on sacred geometry. In phase II, more and more members of living mandalas will ascend and this will trigger an Ascension chain reaction.

**PHASE III:** At some point a critical mass of 144.000 beings will achieve Ascension on this planet. Planetary soul family will live in their light bodies in sacred mandalas, anchoring the Invisible. This will open the Doorway of Ascension and transform the planet into the New Earth. Most beings will continue living on New Earth in paradise; however some will continue their journey to the stars, joining the cosmic brotherhood and Galactic evolution of Oneness.

## LIVING MANDALAS

Cosmic energies of Oneness are coming to Earth through vortices of Ascension. Ascension groups and living mandalas will transmit these energies among population. Living mandalas will distribute the Ascension message among people.

Ascension vortices are oases of New reality. They are energetic dimensional vortices of liquid light. Some Ascension vortices manifest as power spots throughout the planet, some will anchor themselves as living mandalas. Ascension vortices are sixth dimensional angelic beings. These angels transmute duality into Oneness and assist in individual and group Light body activation. They cause gathering of soul families, soul mates and twin souls in living mandalas. They accelerate group initiation and Ascension process. They are like great pumps which can absorb whole groups into world of Oneness.

Ascension vortices are instruments of Divine intervention which break the old reality system of cause and effect (karma) and establish Divine grace. They connect into a pulsating planetary grid of liquid light and through resonance morphogenetic field create a reality shift for this planet.

Living mandalas are physical manifestation of Ascension vortices. They are formed by awakened beings coming together in a clear multidimensional relationship. They are coming together for a purpose of group initiation and Ascension. Group process dramatically accelerates the Ascension path.

Process of raising one's vibration is occurring through spiritual initiations. First initiation means disidentification from your physical body. You do not perceive yourself anymore as physical body. Second initiation means disidentification from your emotional (astral) body. In the past, usually five or more lifetimes used to pass between first and second initiation, but now you can complete this process in few years using Ipsalu tantra technology. Third initiation means disidentification from your lower mental body. From first to sixth sub degree of third initiation you are in a process of purification and disidentification form your causal body. In seventh sub degree of third initiation you don't perceive yourself as causal body anymore; you identify yourself with higher mind (manas). When you reach the door of fourth initiation you come face to face with the dweller of threshold. This means you become more and more aware of implants that you received when you entered third dimension. You need to consciously transform them into light and each part of you must choose Oneness for you to become a fourth degree initiate, a liberated being. This means final purification of your physical, emotional and mental bodies, a time for absolutely positive use of free will. Liberation process is completed through the monadic fire of redemption. So at fourth initiation the purification process is completed, all your bodies are transmuted and you become a pure being of light and love. Then suffering for you doesn't exist anymore. This is liberation. At fifth initiation you master space, time and matter and become a Master of wisdom. This is your goal - Ascension.

When the center of a living Mandala achieves his/her fourth initiation, a pure channel of light and love is established and this harmonizes Mandala greatly. It accelerates group Light body activation and facilitates Ascension process for other members of Mandala.

For living Mandala to function, group merger and synthesis of female and male energies is needed. This causes transition from duality into Oneness. Combination of one being of male polarity in the center of Mandala, surrounded with more beings of female polarity is the most effective. Center of Mandala channels the electric monadic fire of redemption whereas beings surrounding him invoke magnetic energy of solar fire of love.

Living mandalas were brought to Earth in Atlantis through Brotherhood of the star. Brotherhood of the Star is a department of the Ascended master Brotherhood, responsible for anchoring Oneness on this planet. Order of the Star, as a manifestation of the Brotherhood of the Star, created some famous mandalas in Earth history: IS:IS Mandala in Atlantis, .L.U.X.O.R. Mandala in ancient Egypt, Mandala of Jesus and his twelve apostles, Grail Mandala of the round table and shiva-shakti tantric Mandala in Tibet.

One stellar cycle ago, 25.800 years ago, Blue lodge of Sirius sent a wave of star children to Earth. Star children are carrying codes for transition from duality into Oneness in their Light bodies. These codes are being activated now at the completion of the stellar cycle as the world is ready to enter into Oneness. Star children are recognized by the innocence of their inner child. They had very few incarnations on this planet. Star children of all ages are playing a major role in creating living mandalas throughout the planet.

## GROUP MERGER

Group merger is the way of achieving Oneness in a living Mandala. Most people feel that one can be in an intimate relationship only with one person. This perception needs to be explanted, because at this time group consciousness is emerging that will lead to greater love and fulfillment. In world of Oneness beings with common vision are connecting. And if a group of people is aligned with truth, everybody knows his own path which is aligned with the path of the whole.

Intimacy is that brings a living Mandala together: being together, telling the deeper truth, expressing feelings, merging physically. Expressing all energies through One heart in a Group. Merger of soul family with bodies and souls, being close as dolphins on Sirius. There needs to be a yearning in the heart of everybody, a yearning for getting closer and merging.

In a living Mandala beings meet simultaneously as starry angels and as men and women. They heal the separation between heart and sexual energy. They transcend taboos of duality regarding touching and exchange of sexual energy. They do not have any don't touch zones. They manifest and express their divine female and male archetypes. They are open and accepting. They express their sexual energy through open heart and fuse it with energy of Love. Many times it is not needed to express it through a sexual union. Many times it is enough to express it with a gentle touch or a beautiful sensual massage. And it will transform into Love and create a fifth dimensional field of liquid light.

## GROUP MERGER EXERCISE

There is a beautiful exercise which connects the consciousness of a group effectively into One. Let members of the group make a circle and hold their hands. Let them feel how the center of the circle is filled with the essence of Cosmic Love. Let them close their eyes , drop their hands, begin to move towards the center of the circle and meet each other. By gently touching all over their bodies they get to know each other, acquire trust and relax themselves. The whole group then gathers together in the center so that they are totally close together. Then together they breathe in Light, which fills every cell of their bodies. And they can breathe like this for some time and merge consciousness, totally embraced and wrapped into One.

## EXERCISE FOR TANTRIC MERGER

Let a couple stand on front of each other. Feel each other and find the beauty of Divine being in each other. Breathe through your hearts. When you breathe out, breathe out yearnings for merger from your heart and send them towards each other. When you breathe in, breathe in yearnings for merger that you have accepted from each other, into your heart. And when a good contact is established among you, begin to caress each other over your souls and your bodies. Allow all energies to express themselves. Allow the energy of love to flow through you. If you feel any emotional energy allow it to be expressed through yourselves, through your breathing. If you feel sexual energy, allow it to be expressed through your presence, through your breathing, through your heart, through your touch. Members of the group can make a circle around you and hold their hands. They can visualize the energy which flows through their hands in a clockwise direction. So in the middle of the circle your vibration will begin to rise. This type of raising the vibration is known from the time of Atlantis. When the vibration is high enough, the group drops their hands and begins to caress you all over your bodies. Breathe together through your hearts and be in consciousness of Oneness. And when you feel you can finish the exercise.

**Living Mandala is a multidimensional hologram of interconnected soul family, soul mates and twin souls.**

Group merger in a living Mandala begins on a soul family level. Soul family is your true family, your star friends, brothers and sisters. Soul family relationships are formed after first initiation is achieved. Soul family merger creates a field of fifth-dimensional liquid light, the aura of the group Light body. It prepares group Light body for its activation.

Group merger is deepened with deep soul mate relationships. Soul mates are beings of opposite polarity with whom you share alignment of inner being and deep understanding. Stable soul mate relationships are only possible after second initiation is reached. Soul mate merger adds sixth-dimensional magnetic love energy to the living Mandala.

Finally, merger of twin souls into One being is achieved. Twin souls are one soul, incarnating into two bodies of opposite polarity. They are perfect mates for each other. Stable twin soul union is possible after third initiation. Twin soul merger adds seventh-dimensional miraculous energy of Oneness to the living Mandala.

At fourth initiation all energies are expressed and transformed into pure Cosmic love. At this point, group relationship transcends man-woman polarity. Whole group merges into a Cosmic angelic being of light and group Light body is finally activated.

All beings that merge in a living Mandala are multidimensional projections of One divine spark, scattered fragments of starry essence that merge into One again. All these interlocking multidimensional levels of merger create wheels within wheels of spiral movements that create the vortex of Ascension. This vortex serves as a dimensional buffer during your transition from third to seventh dimension and finally triggers group Ascension.

## ISLANDS OF LIGHT

When a living Mandala activates its Light body, it manifests externally as an Island of light. Island of light is a community of Oneness, created in alignment with sacred geometry. It is created as an experience of Heaven on Earth.

All Islands of light will be self-sufficient regarding food, money and energy sources. They will exist outside duality in an oasis of the New reality. In Islands of light people will receive assistance and guidance for their Ascension process. Islands of light will be connected energetically with each other and will create a network of light which will emanate energies of Love and Ascension towards the rest of humanity.

Those who live in Islands of light will demonstrate true Love which emanates from consciousness of Oneness. They will cooperate with Cosmic brotherhood and their lightships which are in fact Islands of light in the sky. Inside Islands of light, individual and group healing of body and soul will be taking place. Use of etheric medicine technology and spiritual powers of healing will allow miraculous healings to occur. Members of Islands of light will discover deeper and deeper levels of merger through the process of Galactic tantra. Scientists will deepen their understanding of Cosmos through the science of vibration of matter. Artists will create multidimensional sculptures from liquid light. Technicians will supply Islands of light with free energy which will be produced from etheric substance (prana). Islands of light will thus serve as models of New reality on Earth.

## CREATION OF MANDALAS

**I) Individual preparations**

Any individual that wishes to be a part of a living Mandala needs to be absolutely devoted to Ascension process. He needs to make an insisting, unconditional and unbreakable decision for his own Ascension, no matter what happens, regardless of external circumstances.

Anybody wishing to join a living Mandala needs to be committed to constant purification of all of his bodies. Physical body is being purified with lots of rest and cleansing with four elements: earth, water, fire and air. Emotional body is being purified by giving loving attention to your emotions. Mental body is purified through triangulation: alternatively making affirmations for a mental pattern and its opposite pattern and finally transcending both towards a higher synthesis. Causal body is transformed by inviting an Ascended master that is closest to you to overshadow it and dwell in it with his presence.

At some point during the purification process you make your final unbreakable decision to join or create a living Mandala. When this decision is made, universe provides you with the next step. This next step is usually Light code activation. You come across some high quality channeled material which awakens your inner knowing. Or you see some drawn mandalas that assist in your awakening.

Cosmic stones such as moldavites or ordinary tektites are excellent tools for Light code activation. All forms of tektites are interdimensional doorways into One. You can arrange them into sacred geometry stone mandalas, which will attract the manifestation of a real living Mandalas to you.

Ordinary black tektites (indochinites) came 870.000 years ago from the AN (Al Nilam) stargate in Orion. They assist in changing reality systems from duality into Oneness. They anchor the first ray, the ray of Divine purpose.

Saffordites and columbianites are tektites of violet-brown colour and came from Sirius. They bring forth energies of Love and Grace and anchor the second ray, the ray of Divine love.

Moldavites are tektites of beautiful green color and came 15 million years ago from AL-TA (Alcyone) star gate in Pleiades. They activate your starry angelic presence and anchor the third ray, the ray of Divine light. Holy Grail is a sacred chalice of the Order of the Star, made of moldavite, which serves as a physical anchor and a coordination point for planetary One living Mandala. Unit mandalas can use pieces of moldavite as a physical anchor and a symbolic representation of the Holy Grail.

**II) Mandala Activation**

When your Light codes are activated, universe provides you with the next step of meeting individuals which are part of your living Mandala. You can meet them in »casual« meetings, in existing groups or by creating your own group. Some enough aware individuals coming to your group can become members of your inner living Mandala. Or you may be even lucky enough to join an already existing living Mandala.

Mandala is activated when three or more beings come together in deep relationship on all planes: spiritual, mental, emotional and physical. Mandala allows no separation on any plane. Members of a living are supporting each other, willing to merge and deepen contact. Before you enter a living Mandala you need to release all relationships that do not bring you happiness, all relationships that block or restrain group Mandala process. Living Mandala requires total sincerity and dedication to group Ascension process from all members. It is good for a living Mandala to meet regularly at least once a week to build up energy and strengthen the connection.

Members of Mandala accept no compromises, they join in higher synthesis. If nobody in Mandala accepts compromises, Mandala will work smoothly, almost miraculously. Any compromises or duality can lower its vibration and make its growth more difficult. Each member of Mandala needs to be sincere with himself and accept responsibility for his shadow side rather than denying it and projecting it to other members of Mandala. Also, living Mandala has no room for jealousy and symbiotic-over dependency type of relationships.

When all these requirements are met, living Mandala can grow and open like a lotus flower. It begins to emanate love outwards and contributes to manifesting Divine plan on Earth.

## MEDITATION FOR MANDALA CREATION

1. Visualize a brilliant twelvefold star in the sky. This star is rotating clockwise with its central point resting in no-time and emanating presence of Oneness.
2. Visualize a gimlet of rainbow light emanating from the center of the star spiraling downwards through your crown, brow and throat chakras into your heart.
3. Visualize a small brilliant twelvefold star in your chest. It is rotating clockwise on a horizontal plane together with the star in the sky. The central point of the star is still, resting in no-time and emanating presence. Feel your yearnings of merging with your soul family, soul mates and your twin soul, let the star in your heart rotate and expand , sending your yearnings and your call outwards. Let it expand beyond your city, your country, your continent and all over the world. Visualize your

beloved soul brothers and sisters respond, come to you and merge with you.

4. Visualize all of you ascending in the star in the sky and merging with Cosmic brotherhood. Merge into One being, travel together in the direction of Orion and enter the stargate of An (middle star in the belt of Orion).
5. Stay on the other side of AN as long as appropriate and close with OM.

# CHAPTER TWO

# THE UNDERGROUND KINGDOM OF LIGHT

In Atlantean times, 25000 years ago, when Earth became a quarantine planet under the occupation of dark forces, one part of forces of light withdrew under the surface and built there a civilization of many cities of light, interconnected with vast system of tunnels. In those Atlantean cities, beings were pursuing their spiritual path under the vigilant guidance of the King of the world, Lord Sanat Kumara. This kingdom of light is known by the name of Agartha or Shamballa and must not be confused with Shamballa which exists on the etheric plane since Lemuria and which served as a spiritual beacon for the underground civilization.

In underground Agartha people lived in harmony between spiritual worlds and advanced Atlantean technology that served for their highest good. Each of them knew his higher purpose and followed it so they lived with each other in harmonious relationships. Until the final deluge of Atlantis they were protected against attacks of the dark forces which have also built their strongholds in certain areas of the underworld since then. After the deluge everything changed. Dark forces began to attack Agartha and as the Tibetan holy book Dzyan said »there were fighting's between builders and destroyers and fighting's for space«. Forces of light were forced to leave many territories which they inhabited before. The system of underground tunnels was encircling the whole planet. The western tunnel network had its beginning under Atacama desert in Chile and went in direction of Tiahuanaco - Cuzco - Mount Shasta - Grand Tetons, under American mainland and under Atlantic ocean towards Atlas mountain range in western Africa and then under Ahaggar/Tibesti mountain ranges towards their final station - the Giza pyramids. One important center was under Mato Grosso region in Brazil, where Agartha had strong connection with Atlantean cities on the surface. The Himalayan network was of extraordinary importance. Here underground civilization developed as a mirror of Atlantean colony which existed on the surface in the area of contemporary Gobi desert. Of course it was no desert then, it was a subtropical paradise. Himalayan network had its source under the Gobi desert and it expanded under Takla Makan desert and then onwards under Pamirs, Altai, Karakorum, Baltistan, under Kunluns and under Chang Tang plateau towards Himalayas.

After the deluge of Atlantis, certain groups on the surface have come across important spiritual and scientific discoveries and have therefore retreated in the underground Agartha from the dark forces which had almost whole surface in their grip by then. These reinforcements have accelerated scientific and technological progress in Agartha and with united forces they have unsealed old Atlantean tunnels, restored old Atlantean machines and expanded original underground spaces in which they dwelt. With those expansions they often followed the course of underground rivers and underground energy streams. Development of technology was outstanding. Beyond old Atlantean crystal technology they were developing teleportation chambers and free energy technology. They have connected their underground cities with trains that used magnetohydrodynamic (MHD) drive, which then reached speeds up to 3,000 mph. They came into touch with the galactic starfleet which has succeeded in rescuing some of them from the quarantine Earth. Resistance movement of the forces of light, which had its starbases on the Moon, Mars, asteroids, moons of outer planets and on planet X was sending in reinforcements all the time.

In time of ancient Greece certain colonists have voyaged across Atlantic to Brazil and US west coast and made contact with Agartha there. Many ancient cultures that vanished without a trace (for example the Mayans) have in fact moved into the Agartha empire. Some Hopi Indians have had contact with Agartha just a few decades ago. In Agartha, Order of the Star was very active. Its purpose is healing of separation on planet Earth and also successful completion of experiment of duality. Kings of Agartha were leaders of the Council of twelve and were a physical anchor for the energies of Sanat Kumara. Certain American presidents and presidents of some other states had contact with kings of Agartha during their term. Agartha often exerted its spiritual influence on the surface, especially the Himalayan network in the region of India and Tibet. Over one thousand years ago, representatives of Agartha near Gilgit in contemporary Pakistan spread tantric teachings to the surface. In nineteenth century they strongly influenced teachings of Helena Petrovna Blavatsky who had physical contacts with them. In the beginning of twentieth century Aagrtha had over twenty million members. During WW 1, invasion of the dark forces begun. They wanted to break the power of Agartha. Hordes of warriors of darkness rolled from enormous bases under China, Indonesia, near East and Africa through tunnels across Atlantic towards Mexico and then southwestern US to limit the spiritual influence of Agartha on arising western civilization. There were severe underground physical battles that mirrored on the surface as WW 1 and WW 2. After victory of the forces of light at the end of WW 2, Agartha turned its attention towards spiritual awakening of the West. Forces of darkness turned their attention to annihilation of Himalayan network which reflected on the surface as Chinese occupation of Tibet. Stroke of the dark forces in 1996 weakened Agartha dramatically and in 1999 Agartha was almost erased from its underground dwellings. Therefore at the end of 1999 very strong reinforcement of forces of light came in the shape of the resistance movement fighters from the asteroid belt and planet X. Planet X has a radius of 9000 miles with a surface of frozen methane that gives it a bluish color. Planet X is orbiting the Sun in very inclined elliptical orbit 6 to 7 billion miles away.

Forces of darkness had their maximum power between 1996 and 2003. Outer part of the dark forces are the Draconians, humanoid beings from Alpha Draconis star system. Since Atlantis they have a plan for mass control of human population, named New World Order. They use world politics to create artificial conflicts between nations and ignite wars to gain profit. Their main centers of activity are in Washington, Brussels and Rome. They enslave humanity with programmable biochips that are inserted into human body with vaccinations, and with nanoelectronic devices that control and direct human thoughts. Through their representatives in church, freemasonry and occult groups they control human spirituality and create spiritual conflicts. Their core is so called Illuminati, a chosen group that has control over the System on Earth. Only Illuminati are directly connected with true masters of the quarantine Earth, a race of creatures which was created millions of years ago by the Dark lords of Orion with genetic engineering. These creatures prevent advanced extraterrestrial civilizations access to Earth, holding humanity as a hostage, threatening with nuclear war. They enslave humanity and keep it in quarantine since Atlantis. This race mostly incarnates in humanoid clone bodies, although their true shape is in a form of various mutations of spiders, beetles, insects, reptiles, worms and serpents. Their only motivation is total control over all Creation, spreading malice, terror and dread. They mostly control humanity with implants that create space/time black hole anomaly and thus deface human consciousness to an unrecognizable extent, confusing human mind and emotions. Implants are programmable crystals that were put into physical and energetic bodies of every single human being on Earth with strong electronic devices. The creature race is maintaining distorted space/time structure with electromagnetic space/time chambers similar to those used in Philadelphia experiment. Most efficiently they retard evolution on Earth with threats and violence, spread by their representatives. They are infiltrated in all pores of human society, pretending to be ordinary people. Using unlawful means, threats and violence they prevent meetings between twin souls. In their secret underground bases they have created sexual traumas to many women with horrible rapes, thus blocking the flow of sexual energy on planet Earth. They also created traumas to produce multiple personality disorders, using victims of this process as slaves. Height of their power has fortunately already passed and forces of light are defeating them step by step.

Forces of light are coming to assist in the shape of seventy million members of resistance movement from planet X. They will cause a change of system on Earth in a near future. Old Asian legend says that warriors of Shamballa will come to the surface and destroy the forces of darkness. Resistance movement has developed advanced technology of teleportation chambers, free energy, cloning and biotechnology as a whole. They have their underground cities mostly under bigger cities of Europe and USA. Their cities are interconnected with MHD drive tube-train system with speeds up to 15,000 mph. Their underground civilization is a successor of the kingdom of Agartha which was almost destroyed in attacks of the dark forces between 1996 and 1999.

The core of the light forces are representatives of Atlantean network. This is a group of few thousand individuals of a very high spiritual vibration that is maintaining the purity of Atlantean legacy permanently since the times of Atlantis itself. Atlanteans have their underground residences on some chosen locations under the Himalayas, under southern California, under some atolls near Tahiti and under Titicaca Lake. They inspire individuals towards their ideals of creating a harmonic society that will be known by the name of New Atlantis.

# JOURNEY INTO THE RESISTANCE MOVEMENT

The main body of the Resistance movement came to Earth from planet X with the aid of teleportation chambers in December 1999. They have settled down in underground bases that were emptied before in severe battles between the dark forces and the remnants of Agartha kingdom and the so called Organization. The Organization was a forerunner for the Resistance movement and was a leading resisting force against the dark ones throughout the human history. Between 1975 and 1999 they had their main command center about one thousand feet below the underground railway system of New York. When the weakened forces of the Organization were refreshed with members of the Resistance movement they renewed together many underground dwellings and moved their main command center to a new location.

Now the Resistance movement has most of its locations under bigger surface cities between 100 feet and 8.6 miles underground. Most locations are between 150 and 1500 feet underground. All their locations are sealed hermetically and isolated from surface influences, such as viruses, dust, polluted air, micro/nanochips... Dwellings are constructed in a specific way to avoid underground structures which were built by the surface civilization for its needs, such as electric installations, water supply systems, underground railway, mining tunnels, military installations, drinking water reservoirs, oil pipelines and drillings, scientific laboratories, installations and drillings...Some most important Resistance movement centers are located under following cities: New York, Los Angeles, Salt Lake City, London, Munich and Ljubljana (in Slovenia). Locations that are close to the surface are sometimes lit by sunlight which is directed there with a special mirroring system. Locations that are in greater depths are lit with a soft dispersed light being emitted from free energy light chambers. Those dwellings are thermally insulated since surrounding rock has a pretty high temperature when more than few miles underground.

The Resistance movement consists of three concentric circles. The inner circle has few dozen members which are leaders of the Resistance movement. Only those with extraordinary skills and talents and those that are willing to accept great responsibilities can qualify for those positions. The middle circle consists of hundreds thousands of members with special gifts for planning, organization, technology research and development, psychology, medicine, healing, spirituality, creativity, art, music...The outer circle are army forces. They are not soldiers as we know them on the surface but experienced interplanetary fighters who do not fight only with blind force but have reached a high level of spiritual development also. Their purpose is to liberate the surface of Earth from the dark forces and to assist humanity in building a new civilization.

Dark forces are still blocking almost all activity of the Resistance movement on the surface with their military superiority. The Resistance movement has means to remove all disease and poverty of humanity and they will use them when military victory over the dark forces will be achieved. The Resistance movement also has vast financial resources of over 100,000 billion dollars. This monetary mass is now blocked but will be used for benefit of humanity with the victory of the Resistance movement.

Money is not needed inside the Resistance movement since they have technology that brings them everything they need in life. They use smaller amounts of money for their surface activities, which are not yet very frequent. Everybody inside the Resistance movement does the work he is most talented for. Nobody is forced to work. Every work is done from an inner need for creation. Talents are encouraged and not suppressed as it is the case on the surface. Artists can create new music or excel in painting or sculpture. There are special museums in middle circle of the Resistance movement with objects of art from Atlantis and other high cultures, especially Greco – Roman culture, that serve as a source of inspiration . Everybody from the Resistance movement has access to important pieces of information which are transmitted from the Pleiadian information network. The basic cell of society is not family as is the case on the surface, but soul family, where people meet and mingle according to soul connections they have. Their relationships are much more open, expression of emotional and sexual energies is allowed. Despite all that their relationships are not completely harmonious since the Resistance movement has not yet recovered completely emotionally from severe battles with the dark forces few years ago.

Science and technology are very developed inside the Resistance movement. The Resistance movement is actively cooperating with the Galactic confederation which has its strongholds throughout the solar system. They use teleportation chambers for long distance transportation, especially for journeys towards the asteroid belt and planet X. The Resistance movement uses materialization chambers to materialize whatever they need from the etheric substance. They use those chambers to make machines, equipment, objects for daily use and food. Some people prefer to prepare food in a traditional way – by growing vegetables and cooking. Free energy chambers are the main source of energy inside the Resistance movement and they produce physical energy out of the etheric substance. This technology is recently being replaced with tachyon energy which is not based upon electromagnetic radiation and is a clear source of energy of light. With tachyon receivers it is possible to permeate the physical matter with tachyons so that it becomes an emitter of pure light. This process is called tachionization. By using this process they make wonderful refreshment drinks and change them into an elixir of life, which rejuvenates cells of their bodies. Cloning technology is developed to its perfection and with its aid everyone can choose a physical body according to his taste. People have no health problems except for occasional symptoms that have emotional origin. Eventual problems with inner organs are not removed with operations but with special materialization chambers. Their biotechnologists have developed so called bioskin that can heal up any physical wound in a few moments. With the use of nanotechnology they have developed miniature robots for removal of viruses and harmful biochips. Their computer programmers have broken into the mainframe computer of the dark forces. This computer has a program that controls thinking processes of humanity with a network of micro biochips that are implanted in the brain of every living human on the surface of the planet. A good example of this program is shown in the Matrix movie. When the program in the mainframe computer will be completely broken, the biochip network will begin falling apart and people will realize in astonishment that they have lived psychologically for years in a virtual world without any real contact with themselves, with each other or with nature and the universe. When was the last time that you have been watching the sunset?

Spiritual guidance of the Resistance movement is the Atlantean network. The Atlantean network also consists of three circles. The inner circle are few dozens of priests from Atlantis that have retreated from the surface 25 thousand years ago. They still have the same physical bodies since they have reached immortality. They were completely isolated for all this time without any contact with the surface in order to preserve the purity of their consciousness. They are the last unchanged remnant from Atlantis. They live together on a specific energy point inside the Himalayas and are connected in a special way with the Great White Brotherhood of Ascended masters and with the Lord of the world, Sanat Kumara. Their purpose is to be an intermediary between the world of Ascended masters and the world of unascended human beings.

The middle circle of the Atlantean network consists of few hundreds beings that have contact only with the inner circle and the Galactic confederation. Their purpose is to preserve the legacy of Atlantis. The outer circle consists of few thousand members that have physical contacts with the Resistance movement and offer them spiritual guidance in the form of a mystery school which is a direct successor of mystery schools of old Atlantis. Sometimes they also influence the surface of the planet by sending spiritual impressions to those humans that are receptive for spiritual guidance from the higher mental plane. In the past some highly developed individuals from the surface were accepted in the middle and outer circle of the Atlantean network. Some of them have already reached their Ascension, some have left the Earth, and some are still part of the Atlantean network. Underground palaces of the Atlantean network are wonderful, adorned with crystals, surrounded with waterfalls and running water. In crystal temples of Atlantean network the legacy of Atlantis is waiting for a time when on the surface it will establish a just world of New Atlantis.

# GALACTIC WARS

Universe came into existence as a result of dynamic tension between the Absolute and contingency. Although the Absolute is eternal, infinite and perfect in the area of meaning, his power is limited with senselessness of contingency as contingency is his logical opposite.

Contingency existed as a potential random wave function, which was manifested into a multidimensional space/time membrane by the will of the Absolute. Universe came into existence inside this membrane. The Absolute intervenes into the universe with his free will (thirteenth ray) which arranges chaotic contingency of the universe into a meaningful whole of twelve rays that represent twelve energetic qualities of the universe. Until recently only seven lower rays, which are quite developed, were known on this planet. But now information about five higher rays is also present. The twelve rays are:

- First ray........will
- Second ray.....love
- Third ray.......creative intelligence
- Fourth ray......harmony
- Fifth ray.........concrete knowledge
- Sixth ray........idealism
- Seventh ray.....manifestation
- Eighth ray......divine grace
- Ninth ray........genius
- Tenth ray........integration
- Eleventh ray....link between dimensions
- Twelfth ray......absolute positivity

Presence of the Absolute in the universe strengthens positivity and supports evolution whereas presence of contingency strengthens negativity and blocks evolution. Therefore negativity and suffering never have a higher purpose as some people erroneously think. Only good can bring about good. Purpose of the Absolute is to permeate contingency with his presence and to lead the evolution of the universe to a point where all contingency will merge with him. The Absolute has chosen Local cluster of galaxies as a sector in the universe where the most negative part of contingency will be resolved. The archidemons were angelic beings who have chosen to delve into the contingency of matter millions years ago in order to transform it with their consciousness. They were carrying this too far and with mutual implantations they lost their awareness and got lost into darkness. Thus dark lords were created. They began to attack planets, to implant and enslave the population there and to create mutant races with genetic engineering. The Ascended masters have limited this infection of darkness to our galaxy and M 31 galaxy in Andromeda. The forces of light have gathered their star fleets and began to liberate infected areas. Thus galactic wars began. The forces of light were most successful in Andromeda galaxy and the forces of darkness were running away into our galaxy. Around the Central sun of our galaxy an advanced civilization came into existence which began to create a Galactic network of light. Galactic legend says that Galactic network of light will be soon completed and then all darkness will vanish from the universe. So dark forces had to run away from the area of light in the center of the galaxy into less evolved surroundings. They have chosen a planet of darkness, orbiting a star named Rigel in Orion as their main stronghold. The central point of darkness was a captured angelic being which was changed into a horseshoe shaped deformed creature with a very powerful implantation process.

Success of the forces of light was such that 25 thousand years main area of darkness was limited to a certain sector of the Galaxy named the Local logos. This is a galactic sector with its centre in the Pleiades and a radius of about one thousand light years. Inside the Local logos, the forces of light had their main centers in the following star systems: Pleiades, Sirius, Hyades, Betelgeuse, EL AN RA stargate in the belt of Orion, Horsehead nebula in Orion, Vega, M 27 planetary nebula in Lyra, Alpha Centauri, Arcturus, Epsilon Eridani and Tau Ceti. The forces of darkness had their main strongholds in the following star systems: Rigel, Alpha Draconis, Zeta Reticuli 1, Zeta Reticuli 2, Epsilon Bootes, Altair, Capella, and Barnard star. Penetration of the light forces had provoked a violent reaction of the dark forces and a mutiny of various mutant races throughout the galaxy which have decided to change planet Earth into quarantine and to use its population as hostages to stop the light forces.

When Earth became a quarantine, Ashtar achieved his ascension with assistance of his living Mandala and thus opened a door to a project of Ascension waves, which will occur at the victory of the light forces on Earth. Ashtar's ascension was the last act of the light forces on Earth before darkness came in. Ascended masters have left the Earth and Atlantean priests have retreated under the surface. Civilization of late Atlantis was decaying on the surface and nobody could escape implantations that were happening over and over again. Soul consciousness of people sank into oblivion. The Blue lodge of Sirius created the Order of the Star 16,000 years ago to stop the decay of Atlantis and heal the separation but this failed and Atlantis was finally destroyed in June 9564 BCE.

The decay continued although divine dynasties of Egypt tried to preserve the tradition of Atlantis. The Central galactic civilization intervened strongly on Earth 3500 years ago and influenced the rise of high culture on Crete. Due to considerable success of this project, the underground Agartha and the Atlantean network decided to actively intervene on the surface and this caused the prosperity of Greco-Roman culture. The Order of the Star used this opportunity and through Jesus tried to awaken humanity for a possibility of Ascension and to create an awareness of the divine plan of ultimate victory over the dark forces.

Forces of darkness reacted strongly and sent reinforcements from the Andromeda galaxy. That caused the fall of the Roman Empire and started a thousand years of darkness in the middle ages. The cosmic turning point, which was set for 11th August 1999 already 25 thousand years ago, began to draw near.

Around the year 1500, which is one half-millennial cycle before the cosmic turning point, the Atlantean network and the underground Agartha caused the bloom of renaissance. Half-millennial cycle of convergence corresponds with seventy weeks of years from an old biblical prophecy.

Around 1750, which is one half of half-millennial cycle before the turning point, the enlightenment movement began to prosper under the influence of Atlanteans and Agarthians. This movement made an attempt to improve the social condition of humanity. Rapid development of science took place that led towards industrial revolution. Dark forces devised a plan for a New World Order as a reaction to that.

One quarter of half-millennial cycle before the turning point, in 1875, Helena Petrovna Blavatsky founded the Theosophical society and thus triggered a spiritual awakening on the surface of the planet. It was then possible for the Ascended masters to influence the planetary situation since people were more aware of their existence. True esoteric knowledge, hidden until then, began to spread among people. WW 1 was a reaction of the dark forces on this awakening.

In 1937, which is one eighth of half-millennial cycle before the turning point, the dark forces wanted to prevent a new awakening and prepared WW 2. When this war was over, the light forces have cleared vast sectors of the Galaxy and the Galactic Confederation began to actively intervene in the consciousness of humanity with new teachings and appearances of UFOs.

In 1968, which is one sixteenth of half-millennial cycle before the turning point, a spiritual awakening happened in the shape of hippie movement and the sexual revolution. This was the peak period of American space program, which is the greatest publicly known achievement of Earthlings in the area of space exploration. As a reaction of the dark side a stroke of Andromedan dark forces happened in 1975 which caused a downfall of the hippie movement and almost destroyed the space program. Other consequences of this stroke were not publicly seen, although they were even more painful. Through the intervention of the Absolute on 25th May 1975 a cosmic doorway opened on Earth, which began to transform darkness of this planet.

1/32 of half-millennial cycle before the turning point, at the end of 1983, the Absolute has revealed a vision of the end of linear space/time continuum to certain individuals and thus anchored the time axis of eternity on this planet. On 17th August 1987 hundreds thousands individuals have opened the doorway of Harmonic convergence, which strengthened a connection between the Galactic confederation and Earth. The Absolute has set planet Earth in the center of his attention by opening a dimensional doorway which causes a lifting of planetary consciousness from the third towards the fifth dimension between 1987 and 2012.

1/64 of half-millennial cycle before the turning point, on 11th January 1992, multitudes of star people have opened the doorway of 11:11. Through eleven gates of 11:11 the Absolute will anchor higher aspects of the first eleven rays. Between 1994 and 1996 there was a time window for a possibility for the first wave of Ascension. The probability of success was around 40%

and Ascended masters did everything to make this happen. But incarnated star beings on Earth decided with their free will mainly against the Ascension waves, the key individuals have accepted incorrect decisions and so the critical mass had not been achieved. Whole project was thus postponed to a period after the public physical contact with extraterrestrial civilizations. This will ease decision for many and critical mass will be easily achieved. With the purpose of preventing the entry of humanity into a New age a cosmic stroke of evil forces happened on 11th January 1996. This was the most terrible attack on Earth in the last 25 thousand years. There was a nuclear war on etheric and astral plane that luckily did not spread towards the physical plane, since humanity used its free will to say no to a nuclear war on the physical plane. This cosmic stroke of the forces of evil has almost destroyed light on Earth. All remaining anomaly of the universe was streaming towards the Earth through infected Local logos. Other sectors of the Galaxy and the rest of the universe were being liberated from darkness and were in their final purification. On 17th May 1998 the winter solstice point on the ecliptic has crossed the galactic equator. That only happens once in 25 thousand years so this was the end of the previous and beginning of the next 25 thousand years cycle.

On 11th August 1999 at the total solar eclipse a cosmic turning point occurred in the form of the fourth gate of 11:11. The Absolute transmitted then a special key to the universe, a key called the New heaven. This key is a tool which enables the universe to purify itself from the darkness completely. At the fourth gate of 11:11 this key has completely purified the whole universe except the Local cluster of galaxies.

In December 1999 a mutiny against the dark forces happened on planet X and in few weeks of severe fighting planet X was liberated on 21st December 1999. Many members of Resistance movement have come to Earth into the underground where they are waiting for the right moment to liberate Earth as well.

By using the key of New heaven the whole Local galactic cluster was purified from darkness on 25th March 2001, except our particular solar system. At the activation of the fifth gate of 11:11 on 19th October 2002 the Absolute began to transmit a new key to the universe, named New Earth. This key is a sub-key to a key of New heaven and is a tool for purification from darkness for planet Earth. Next part of this key was received at the activation of the sixth gate of 11:11 which happened in May 2004.

Harmonic concordance in November 2003 marks the end of absolute rulership of dark forces on Earth which lasted seven years, beginning on 11th January 1996 and reaching its maximal intensity in summer 1999 around the fourth gate of 11:11. These seven years of darkness are mentioned in many old prophecies and have caused ultimate purification of the universe and concentration of remaining darkness around Earth, where it will be cleared until 21st December 2012, when the Absolute will transmit the last part of the key of New Earth.

# LIBERATION OF THE PLANET EARTH

Universe, which is now outside this solar system already free from the anomaly of darkness, is governed by different physical laws than in vicinity of Earth. Basic subatomic particles that transmit information there are not photons but tachyons. Tachyons are subatomic particles that have almost infinite speed and therefore enormous energy and are carriers of the thirteenth ray. Photonic universe is limited with the speed of light and is under the influence of anomaly of darkness, contracting into one single spot - planet Earth. With the speed of light as the maximal possible speed of information transmission the picture of the universe that beings receive is inevitably distorted. Therefore people on Earth cannot easily get a clear picture about what is really going on in this universe.

Between tachyonic and photonic universe the Ascended masters have set a tachyonic membrane which transmits subtle signals from liberated universe into photonic form that human eyes and scientific instruments can perceive. Certain tachyons nevertheless reach Earth and bring realizations about higher dimensions and distant worlds to spiritually developed individuals. Certain quartz crystals, certain opals and specifically treated glass can act as tachyon containers and thus increase concentration of tachyons on the physical plane.

There are many energetic membranes around Earth that demark areas of different stages of purification. Closer to Earth we are, more physical and energetic pollution and anomaly is present. The first of those membranes is about 214 thousand miles above Earth surface just inside lunar orbit and demarks the border between interplanetary space of the solar system and sub lunar space close to Earth. At 137 miles altitude there is a membrane which demarks a border between sub lunar cosmic space and upper Earth atmosphere. This is the lowest point of orbits for almost all artificial satellites. There is also a matrix which creates an energy field of twelve zodiacal signs that represent the foundation of astrology since Atlantis. The last membrane is 8.6 miles above the surface and marks the upper edge of influence of the New World Order. This altitude is determined with maximal altitude of commercial aircraft flights. Higher altitudes are almost unreachable for an average individual except for huge amounts of money.

Universe which is liberated from anomaly of darkness is an area of pure light, love and harmony. Its evolution is guided by the Ascended masters in alignment with the Galactic codex. Galactic codex is in line with inner sense of every being which has known the higher reality. All beings in the liberated universe act with their free will in alignment with the Galactic codex which regulates all their relationships so that they never lead to conflicts. Galactic codex enables every being in the universe with the right for divine grace, which is given to evolving beings by the Ascended masters based on power that the masters have over matter which is freed from anomaly of darkness. Every being in the universe has a right for physical abundance and unlimited spiritual growth which is crowned with the Ascension. Every being in the universe has a right for freedom of movement and a right to be informed about everything in the universe. Every being in the universe has a right to merge with any other being according to closeness of both souls since every being in the liberated universe has chosen Oneness unconditionally with his free will. The One is the future of the universe which leads the evolution of the universe into Oneness with reverse time/space loops. The One is universe as it will evolve in the next cosmic cycle and can be seen as a rainbow structure of amazing beauty by the seer.

In the unliberated sector of the universe the Galactic codex regulates activities of the Galactic confederation in saving humanity. Non-intervention of Galactic confederation is a misinformation, which is being spread by the dark forces. The truth is that the Galactic confederation must be very careful with its actions since the dark forces have taken Earthlings as hostages. The Galactic codex requires fast and effective intervention of the light forces on Earth since many galactic laws are obviously broken by the dark forces, for example with wars, violence, artificially created poverty, hunger, diseases, lack of freedom, censorship of information...This means that Galactic confederation will take over the area of infringement and restore galactic legality regardless of local laws that are currently active on Earth. At a certain point this means that each individual that will refer to the Galactic codex with his free will experience an intervention of the Galactic confederation in his life. When the critical mass of people will make that choice, great social changes will occur. Galactic codex gives a right to every living being for a protection against any negativity from any other living being. Beings of darkness that will choose not to stop spreading negativity when they will be given loving guidance and assistance in spiritual growth will be disintegrated in the Galactic central sun and changed into the basic elemental essence. All other beings will be accepted into the harmonious reality of the liberated universe.

Each individual can contribute towards better circumstances on Earth by supporting the Galactic codex with her/his decision, will and actions. If he supports his/her right for free exit and reentry from/to planet Earth, his/her right to be informed, her/his right for spiritual and physical abundance and his/her right for contact with advanced extraterrestrial civilizations, he/she assists in destroying the implant grid which was created among people in Atlantis in the head area. This implant grid has created the quarantine. If an individual supports her/his right for free flow of love and sexuality he/she assists in destroying the implant grid in the abdomen area which was also created in the time of Atlantis. This implant grid has destroyed almost all man/woman relationships since Atlantis. By destroying this implant grid we can create harmonious relationships and abundance on Earth. The system of New World Order is based on control of sexual and emotional energy. There are many beings of darkness on the astral plane that are controlling and destroying relationships by the use of magical rituals and sophisticated spiritual technology. So people on Earth follow the System too much and there are not enough rebels and revolutionaries that would break the status quo and become the driving force of evolution.

Despite the apparent lethargy there will be a breakthrough which is best described with a physical phenomenon, called the phase transition. This happens when a certain physical system receives a critical amount of energy and suddenly its structure changes drastically. Change of liquid water into vapor by a certain temperature is an example. Such phase transition will happen to society structure on Earth when the Resistance movement will gain enough power to penetrate to the surface and give humanity assistance in technology, healing, information etc. This will cause a stock market crash and fall of the unjust System. Use of nanotechnology, materialization chambers and free energy will mean abundance and well being for everybody. The Pleiadians will reveal themselves to humanity and will show the way towards a Greater reality. With their tachyon technology of light they will create anchors for entry into the higher dimension which will cause the arrival of the Ascended masters. The Ascended masters will carry out the plan of three Ascension waves and the Evacuation of mankind in the time span of a few years. At the time of Evacuation the Earth will undergo its physical transformation and become a planet of light. At that moment all cosmic anomaly of darkness will vanish completely and New Atlantis will be born on Earth, a civilization of light, oneness and harmony. This will most likely happen until 21st December 2012.

# GALACTIC CODEX

Planet Earth is the last planet in this universe under the occupation of the Dark Forces, the last relic of galactic wars that raged throughout the galaxy for millions of years.

As the Galaxy was being liberated form the grip of the Dark Forces, the Forces of Light have been evolving from a military force created in the urgent need to defend basic liberties of sentient beings towards a harmonious galactic and cosmic society. As beings within the Galactic Confederation have evolved spiritually and made their alignment and union with the Ascended Masters, they have discovered an inner codex that regulates all inter-relationships between beings of Light and their relation towards the Dark Forces and occupied planets. This codex is called the Galactic Codex and represents the legal basis for all actions of the Confederation in this and other galaxies. This Codex is not a rigid set of external laws but a systematized code of inner ethics of all souls of Light that all beings of Light accept with their free will because it reflects their inner truth.

We will now state the Galactic Codex in a form that is understandable to an average awakened being in a human society.

***Section I: The Law of Divine Grace:**

**Each sentient being has an inalienable and unconditional right to positive life experience**

To explain Section I we need to understand that suffering and pain have no value in enlightened Galactic society liberated from the influence of Dark Forces and other aspects of cosmic anomaly. To value pain, suffering and sacrifice as a part of the growth experience was a part of the programming from the Dark Forces in order to enslave the population of the occupied planets more easily.

Unconditional positive life experience of every sentient being in the liberated universe is guaranteed from the inner connection of every living being with the Source and strengthened by the power of Ascended Masters over matter which allows them to assist all living beings in their aspirations towards the Source and provide them with necessities of life. Life was never meant to be hard work and struggle but rather a journey of joy and creativity. Different subsections of Section I regulate all life in a liberated universe and all relationships between beings of Light so that conflicts never need to occur. Let us explain the subsections:

*Section I/1: Each sentient being has an inalienable and unconditional right to physical and spiritual abundance

This subsection guarantees a positive life experience for every being in the liberated universe. The Ascended Masters provide for all necessities of living and for physical and spiritual richness and beauty using the power they have over redeemed matter of the liberated universe.

*Section I/2: Each sentient being has an inalienable and unconditional right to Ascension.

This subsection explains how the Ascended Masters use their advanced understanding of spiritual technology of

Ascension and by utilizing the Electric Fire of redemption assist all beings that free-willingly choose Ascension.

*Section I/3: Each sentient being has an inalienable and unconditional right to merge with other beings in proportion with his/her position in the Soul Family Mandala.

This subsection is an instrument of regulation of all relationships inside a Soul Family. It guarantees the merging of beings of opposite polarity (twin souls, soulmates) and alignment of all other beings regardless of their state of development and outer conditions.

*Section I/4: Each sentient being has an inalienable and unconditional right to all information.

This subsection is a guarantee that all beings receive all pieces of information they need to understand their role in the universe, greater perspective of evolution and all other pieces they need for their decisions, growth and well being. All this data is provided by Ascended Masters or other beings that supervise the evolutions of various races and civilizations.

*Section I/5: Each sentient being has an inalienable and unconditional right to freedom.

This subsection provides that every being has an unlimited potential of growth and life experience. Since all beings in the liberated universe create only positivism, their freedom never opposes the freedom of other beings.

***Section II: The Law of Dividing the Conflicting Parties:**

**Each sentient being has an inalienable and unconditional right to be divided and protected from the negative actions of other sentient beings**

This section regulates the conditions in those sections of the universe that have just been liberated from the influence of the Dark Forces but that have not yet been accepted in the Confederation. It requires that the Forces of Light always divide the parties in conflict to protect them from producing mutual harm to each other. Then the Light Forces mediate the conflict until it is resolved. This section is often used to end wars and other armed conflicts.

***Section III: The Law of Balance:**

**Each sentient being that has chosen to live and act against the principles of Galactic Codex and refuses to, or is not able to, accept them now and balance the consequences of the past actions will be taken to the Central Sun, restructured into the basic elemental essence and begin a new cycle of evolution afresh**

This section regulates the relations between the Forces of Light and the Forces of Darkness. When defeated, beings that belong to the Forces of Darkness are given the opportunity to accept the Galactic Codex, do the best they can to correct the mistakes they made and to live positively afterwards. If they accept, they are forgiven and join the Confederation. If they are unable or unwilling to accept, they are taken to the Central Sun, their personalities and soul essences are restructured with the Electric Fire and their divine sparks begin a new cycle of evolution.

***Section IV: The Law of Intervention:**

**The Galactic Confederation has an inalienable and unconditional right to the intervention in all situations where the Galactic Codex is violated, regardless of the local laws**

This section describes the policy of the Light Forces regarding occupied planets. The Confederation reserves the right to intervene in all areas, civilizations, planets or solar systems where the Galactic Codex is violated. It has the right to do so regardless of the position of the local civilizations about this intervention. It always has the right to use all peaceful means of education and regulation. If the critical mass of the Galactic Codex principles is violated, it has the right to use military force. Special cases are planets under direct occupation of the Dark Forces. The Dark Forces usually take the local population hostage to hinder the progress of the Forces of Light. On Earth they threaten with nuclear war if the Light Forces would intervene. This is the main reason why the Light Forces have not yet liberated this planet (and not the so called *we-will-not-intervene-because-we-respect-free-will, we-will-just-watch-as-the-suffering-goes-on* nonsense). As in any hostage situation, this requires a lot of skillful negotiation and tactical approach. This situation is slowly being resolved and planet Earth will be liberated during the course of our lives.

*Section IV/1: Each sentient being has an inalienable and unconditional right of calling upon the Galactic Confederation in need and the Galactic Confederation has the right to assist, regardless of local laws

This subsection gives a legal basis for intervention and assistance to all hostages of the Dark Forces. The Forces of Light always do the best they can to assist and improve the living conditions of all sentient beings, even on Earth. The situation on planet Earth just indicates how much more power has the darkness over the Light on this planet. Fortunately, this will change soon.

*Section IV/2: The Galactic Confederation has an inalienable and unconditional right to the implementation of the Galactic Codex and of conquering the areas of Galactic Codex violation with military force if necessary

This subsection gives a legal basis for the liberation of the occupied planets with military force. The military forces of the

Confederation remove the representatives of the Dark Forces and set the hostages free. Then other Confederation forces guide the process of acceptance of the planet into the Confederation by instructing the local population.

Perhaps some humans feel that the Confederation has no right to intervene and that humanity has the right to solve its problems by itself. This is simply not true. Many wars all over the planet and constant abuse of basic human rights have proven that humanity is not capable of handling its own situation. So it is much better that it receives wise guardians to guide it. The Confederation will also replace the current masters of the puppets (Dark Forces) that humanity has invited long ago in Atlantis. Then the Galactic Codex will finally become the universal code of ethics throughout the universe and darkness will be no more.

# THE GODDESS RETURNS

After many millennia the Goddess is coming back. Her energy is coming slowly, almost without notice, but some day it will overflow the world. Her silent underground flow is slowly quenching the thirst that has accumulated in hearts of men without anybody noticing. A thirst that nothing else can quench. Not prayer. Nor meditation. Or complicated yogic exercises. Nor reading holy books of ageless wisdom. Not thousand experiences that the world can offer.

Goddess was screaming under the heel of patriarchal world for millennia. So much time has passed that everybody forgot that she ever existed. Her pale reflection was seen sometimes on dusty statuettes in forgotten museum depots. Or in the rainbow sparkling water drops of a waterfall in the Amazonian jungle, far away from human world. Or in the lovers' eyes in those moments of no time after their union. Or in the movements of a dancing girl, when nobody can see her.

Lack of feminine softness in a harsh male world has created a disbalance that thrust this world towards a brink of extinction. And now, as the patriarchal system is slowly falling apart, a memory returns from the cracks in the matrix. A memory of paradise that once was, a paradise that will be again...

In Neolithic times of old Europe, worship of healing powers of the Goddess has maintained civilization in equilibrium for hundreds of generations. The Goddess was the source of everything that ever was, a mother, a nurturer, a keeper of life, bearer of cycles of life and death. In holy caves and sacred groves intimate rituals were taking place as a gift to the Goddess. Ancient peoples were marking natural cycles of equinoxes and solstices with celebrations and festivals of sexual love, birth and spiritual renewal. Initiation into the mysteries of the Goddess was usually taking place in an underground cave, cavern or similar underground space by walking through a labyrinth and then through a ritual of merger of the Goddess and the Horned God in the center of the labyrinth. Labyrinth symbolically represented a map of human inner world and the spiritual path, a mandala of human soul, whereas the ritual of merger of Goddess and God represented the merger of female and male principles in the human psyche.

Priestesses of the Goddess were guardians of time. Time was flowing spirally, through natural exchange of seasons, through holy moments of sunrises and sunsets. Triplicity of the Goddess, reflected in the phases of the moon, showed itself in the life of women as an archetype of the maiden, the mother and the crone. The maiden is a symbol of life itself, the mother is the one that gives life and the crone is the symbol of death. Thus the triple Goddess sensibly shows the natural cycle of life and death, when death is just a door into a new life.

Also, priestesses of the Goddess were guardians of life energy. This life energy manifested in two ways. First it was the energy of fertility which brought new physical life and also it was the energy of sexual love which brought new spiritual life. In Neolithic times all society was permeated with both energies of life, therefore it was a happy society and knew happiness that modern man has lost.

But this paradise did not last forever. At the end of Neolithic era rough Kurgan warriors on their horses invaded from beyond the Caucasian steppe into the old Europe. They hated the Goddess. They hated the woman and her sexuality and were destroying it with brutal rapes. They have created hierarchy and patriarchal society as we know it now. They brought wars and violence that peaceful Neolithic peoples, worshippers of the Goddess, did not know how to resist. They were subjugated. But their belief and faith in the Goddess was strong and it carried on for millennia. Priestesses of the Goddess were active in Sumeria as naditu, priestesses of love that were not allowed to marry, but were working instead in the temple as healers and initiators of living sexual energy. This tradition carried on into Assyria and Babylon, wherefrom it reached Semitic peoples. The priestesses were active among Jews as quadesha and among Greeks as hierodulai.

The last strike to the energy of the Goddess came from institutional Christianity when in the year 395 a Roman emperor named Theodosius forbade all pagan rituals and when fanatical monks in black hoods with glassy eyes and foamy mouths started erasing the pagan temples, demolishing the statues, destroying the holy groves, raping the priestesses. The Christian symbol of a suffering man, tortured and put on a cross has replaced the soft, inviting and sensual body of the Goddess for a very long time.

But now the Goddess returns. In the last few decades a new impulse of feminine energies is coming from the depths of space and it is bringing the world back into equilibrium. These new energies have triggered many new spiritual movements such as hippie movement in the sixties, rebirth of neopaganism and widespread interest for spirituality. Many women have rediscovered the Goddess inside of their being and began working as priestesses again.

The Goddess returns. In her sacred groves the spring is coming back. Water from her healing springs will begin to round weary human bodies and souls. In underground caves and caverns rituals dedicated to the Goddess are happening again. And I call you, o pilgrim on the path of Light, to join them.

# SOUL FAMILIES AND 2012

The world you are living in is getting closer and closer towards a total change. First signs of that change are already here. The world financial crisis is a result of the influx of strong cosmic energies from Galactic central sun that are transmitted through the outer planets of our solar system, especially involving Pluto. These energies enter our planet and bring to the surface everything that was hidden and suppressed. Inside the increased vibration of those new energies, an exploitative system such as exists now on our planet can not exist much longer. The financial crisis will continue up to the point where humanity will be forced to establish a system of exchange that will be fair to everybody. 2009 is the last year when things will be "business as usual". Already next year the changes will most likely get more physical and all this will lead towards a culmination point in 2012, when there will be a sudden shift of realities for the whole planet into a more positive future.

These cosmic energy changes will lead individuals to face their fears and look more deeply inside into what they did not wish to see before. This will be the greatest spiritual crisis that humanity has ever experienced. But this crisis is the only way for us as human beings to stop behaving like sheep and finally become beings of Light as was always our higher purpose.

Purification of darkness has come to the point where those who are willing can now begin to create **areas of light**. They will be created first in consciousness, in our interconnectedness. This interconnectedness was not possible in our old world. In our old world we were connecting with each other from the perspective of personality families. In the new world we will connect with each other as soul families. Only areas of light that we will create with interconnectedness will enable a soft transition into the new age when the financial system, which was established by occupying forces on our planet eons ago, finally crashes.

Personality family as a basic cell of society is one of main illusory ideas that was implanted into humanity in the time of Atlantis. This idea caused a shift of focus of consciousness from the soul plane towards the personality plane and also caused the creation of relationships based on genetics, which led to corruption of the genetic blueprint of humanity. If the energies of the soul do not enter the twelve stranded etheric DNA, higher spiritual abilities begin to deteriorate and an illusory matrix is created which changes the life experience into a labyrinth.

Soul family in a physical incarnation is always created by its members recognizing each other as souls, especially by recognizing their own position in the soul family mandala and becoming aware of the nature and purpose of their interrelations. When a soul family is created on a physical plane, this automatically triggers the Ascension process, a process of lifting the vibrational frequency of all its members into the fifth dimension.

For this process to occur there must be a connection between members of the soul family on all planes of creation. Most important is the soul connection that is conscious to the extent that it is recognized by the physical brain of all soul family members. On the mental plane this connection manifests as a free flow of ideas, understanding and pure communication between members of the soul family. On the emotional plane this connection shows as a free flow of emotional energy, clear emotional expression and empathy between all members. On the physical plane it manifests as expression of love through action, loving touch and clear flow of sexual loving energy between members of opposite polarity.

On the soul plane there are different levels of interconnectedness between various members of the soul family. Connections between twin souls are the strongest, but they will begin to be established only after the First Contact between our planetary civilization and extra planetary forces of light. Connections between soul mates are also very powerful. There is a certain electromagnetic attraction that occurs between soul mates and it enables the transformation of all suppressed and unconscious sub personalities. There is also an underlying basic connection between all members of the soul family, between all sisters and brothers of light. This connection is based upon common purpose and a common role in manifesting divine missions that we were born for.

Interactions inside the soul family create wheels within wheels of spiral vortex movements that create a transition bridge between our third dimensional world and worlds of fifth, sixth and seventh dimensions. These spiral vortices activate our light body and serve as a platform for our transition into the new state of consciousness.

Indigo and rainbow children of the new generation inside a soul family will not be brought up only by their genetic parents, but by the whole community instead, so they will grow into much healthier individuals. Sexual energy, suppressed by religions for millennia and manipulated by modern media, will finally be released and connected with the energy of the soul. Women will discover again their role as goddesses, liberate their sexuality, connect it with the soul and begin to heal with it. Men will again become visionaries, heroes and builders of the new world. Monogamy will not be the only way of relating between men and women anymore, but only one of the options.

When we will create enough areas of light through our soul family interconnections and when our financial system will reach a critical point of decay, soul families will begin to decide to physically live together and will begin to create **communities of light**. Those will learn how to act according to the principles of higher consciousness. When this consciousness will be developed enough, those communities will grow into **islands of light**. Islands of light will be spots on the planet that will establish First Contact with extra planetary forces of light. These light forces will quench all remaining military conflicts and introduce an era of peace to humanity. It will be the dawning of the new age, the age of Aquarius...

# THE COMING YEARS

Year 2012 will be marked by extremely increased solar activity. Solar activity maxima usually occur every 11 years and they represent a doorway through which the Galactic consciousness is entering the solar system. Energies of the Galactic central sun always cause drastic changes in the human society.

If we take a look at how Galactic impulses at solar activity maxima have influenced humanity, we see an astounding picture. The solar maximum in 1778 has triggered the American Revolution and signing the Declaration of Independence just two years before. The maximum of 1788 has triggered the French revolution in 1789, which is a mere year after that. At the solar maximum of 1804 Napoleon became the French emperor. The maximum of 1816 happened just one year after the Vienna congress which changed the political shape of Europe. The maximum of 1830 was marked by the June revolution in France. The maximum of 1848 is a great milestone since it was the time of March revolution which removed feudalism from most of Europe. The solar maximum of 1860 has triggered the unification of Italy into an unified state just a year later. The next maximum in 1871 is known for the Parisian Commune. The maximum of 1883 triggered the volcanic eruption of Krakatoa, the greatest volcanic eruption in modern era, whereas the next maximum in 1893 caused the crash of New York stock market.

The next maximum in 1907 triggered the first Russian revolution that was taking place between 1905 and 1907. The maximum of 1917 caused the October revolution in Russia.. The solar maximum of 1928 triggered the famous stock market crash of 1929, the biggest stock market crash up to date. The next maximum of 1937 influenced the rise of fascism and consequentially the start of the World War II, through which a vast portion of Galactic darkness was purified. The solar maximum of 1947 triggered the Informbiro of the Stalinist regime the year after. The next maximum in 1957 influenced the beginning of the space age with the launch of the first orbital satellite. On political plane it triggered the Soviet occupation of Hungary the year before and also the Cuban revolution. The maximum of 1968 is known for the hippie sexual revolution, whereas the maximum of 1980 was relatively peaceful, if we don't take the eruption of St. Helens volcano into account. The next maximum in 1991 triggered the collapse of communist regimes in Eastern Europe. The solar maximum of 2001 is world famous for 9-11. So what awaits us at the next maximum in 2012?

Astronomers predict this to be the strongest solar maximum in the last 50 years. Besides that, a Galactic cycle will end then which will trigger a strong eruption of energies from the Galactic central sun that will travel to Earth via Jupiter. The energies coming in between 2009 and 2012 will trigger the final purification of darkness of this planet. In 2010 the energies will be strong enough to start a new wave of mass awakening, similar to the one that was happening in early 90s. The changes will start getting more and more physical and more and more people will realize that something extraordinary is going on. The system of control that was put up in Atlantis by the dark forces will hopefully finally crumble and give space for humanity to create something new, something better. After 2012 these energies will be so strong that they could enable the First Contact between Earth humanity and extraterrestrial civilizations. First, the Pleiadians will appear to humanity. They watch over the destiny of mankind since Atlantis, when they built the foundation of civilization on Earth. Since Atlantis many Pleiadians acted as spiritual teachers on Earth. This time the Pleiadians will appear en masse.

They will bring the light of truth to humanity and it will shine as a guide through intensive changes that await our planet. After 2012 the energies form the Galactic central sun will namely flow uninterrupted and they will cause drastic changes. They will trigger uninterrupted increased solar activity which will cause extraordinary temperature and climate changes on the surface of the planet. Due to increased temperatures enormous stock of methane hydrate above Arctic Circle will melt. It will act as a greenhouse gas and raise the temperature additionally, which will cause accelerated melting of Arctic and Antarctic ice shelves and thus massive flooding of coastal areas. Water will drown all coastal cities and this will trigger mass migrations towards higher grounds. But because dark forces will not be present then anymore and since the whole process will be taking place under direct guidance of the forces of light, those changes will not be as stressful as they could be otherwise. Therefore we can expect such a fast rising of consciousness that the first wave of Ascension could happen around 2016, the second wave around 2020 and the third wave around 2025 along with the mass evacuation of humanity. 2025 is the year when the Earth is supposed to complete its transition into the fifth dimension and through the physical polar shift become a sacred planet with hyper dimensional consciousness.

The year 2025 marks the completion of a 50 year cycle that started in 1975 and it represents a dimensional doorway through which the absolute will transform all darkness of the universe and will help Earth in its transition into the fifth dimension. This is the most intensive period in our whole incarnational cycle and let's do our best since opportunity like this one only occurs once in millions of years. So let us travel together in the new world that is being born....

# VISION 2012

It will begin suddenly, without warning. Many scandals that will disclose true background about how the System works will shake human masses. Disclosures about how international energetic mega companies earn billions selling oil, preventing at the same time inventions of free energy to come to public. Disclosures about pharmaceutical trusts that earn money with »healing« diseases that are spread with viruses created in hidden laboratories. Disclosures about efficient cures for AIDS, cancer and other diseases that are known for quite some time, unknown to human masses. And about world media and censorship there, which is a logical consequence of a fact that few individuals own most worldly known newspaper, media and telecommunication companies. And finally disclosures about a secret world government that has most prominent politicians as its puppets and which creates profit out of wars and human suffering for millennia, a small group of beings that you work for in your jobs and voluntarily give them a significant amount of your monthly salary.

When lists with names, supported with facts will be known, human masses will arise. When facts will be known about what is happening in the stock market and where the money really goes, this will create a world stock market crash and fall of the current monetary system. Riots will begin as a consequence of released emotional energy which was suppressed for so long. In the chaos of those days members of the Resistance movement will reveal themselves to humanity and give guidance and support. They will penetrate to the surface from their underground realms and bring along technology that will help humanity to get over those critical moments. They will cure most of currently known diseases with their medicaments.

With their free energy sources they will end world energy crisis and stop environmental pollution. They will bring information that will open the eyes of people. Finally people will realize that they have lived in quarantine for millennia. Money will disappear and will be replaced with exchange of goods based upon vibrational economy. The Resistance movement will assist in establishing new world government which will be chosen by humanity with its free will and that will lead humanity based on the principles of the Galactic codex. At that point the energy field of the planet will be cleared significantly. Memories of Atlantis will be returning to people and they will begin to create a New Atlantis, a new civilization of light. Buildings will be constructed in a combination of Atlantean and modern architecture which will be in harmony with nature. Many will be in a pyramidal or half spherical shape. Spiritually developed individuals will begin to gather in New age communities, so called islands of light. Everybody there will follow his vision aligned with the divine plan in deep connection with the universe. When people will release the past, everybody will experience clarity of mind, emotional aliveness and physical health. The basic cell of society in islands of light will not be a family of personalities (father, mother and children) but a family of souls (twin souls, soul mates and other members of a soul family). People will connect there energetically and telepathically with angels, guides and extraterrestrials. Through islands of light a physical connection between the surface of the planet and extraterrestrial civilizations will be established. There will be teleportation chambers in islands of light through which it will be possible to travel into the Resistance movement, for some people into the Atlantean network and also towards the Pleiadian mother ships. When the network of light will be strong and stable enough this will enable mass landings of Pleiadian starships. The Pleiadians will assist humanity during its transition towards the New age and with the process of acceptance of this planet into the Galactic confederation. They will anchor energy columns that will guide planet Earth through its transformation during its entry into the inner section of the tachyon belt.

When the critical mass of consciousness will be achieved the first wave of Ascension will occur. Mother ships of the Galactic confederation will hover as brilliant white clouds above the islands of light, where teleportation beams will descend and lift the volunteers into the mother ships. Those volunteers will reappear on Earth shortly in Ascended state in their rainbow bodies of light. Soon afterwards another critical mass will be achieved and the second wave of Ascension will happen. Masses of Ascended masters that will return to Earth will prepare humanity for the third wave of Ascension and for the Evacuation. Great planetary cataclysms will begin then as a cleansing of the physical matter of the planet. At the moment of most intensive cataclysms a polar shift will happen and that will trigger the third wave of Ascension with final Evacuation. Linear time as we know it will end and Earth will enter a new, higher dimension...

# END

# INTERVIEW WITH ISHTAR ANTARES

When in 1993 in one of the Slovene New age magazines an article about the evacuation of mankind in space ships has been published, Ishtar Antares from Ljubljana came to see. He said that he has knowledge about the evacuation of mankind since his childhood.

## HOW WILL SPACE PEOPLE RESCUE EARTHLINGS?

It will happen in three waves. Upon the first wave about 1000 to 2000 people will be taken to space ships - these are STAR PEOPLE, who came from the stars. Those among them who are the most aware, who had released all attachments towards the Earth and know what there is to do, will go first. Upon the ships they would achieve their full consciousness, the consciousness of Ascended Masters. By their free will they will return to Earth and help carry out the evacuation till its end. Some of them will return, some of them will not, mostly they will. Those will prepare the second wave. At that time at least 144.000 beings will be evacuated - this is the critical mass for humanity. That number of Ascended Masters needs to be here upon the Earth to save mankind. And they will return to Earth as Masters to prepare the third wave. The third wave will be evacuated right before the major catastrophe, or cataclysm.

## DOES THE DATE OF CENTRAL POINT OF EARTH TRANSFORMATION THE 11TH of AUGUST 1999 AGREE WITH SOMETHING?

This date agrees with everything. This is a time of the total solar eclipse, at 11 hours 11 minutes. In Ljubljana, the Sun will be, at that moment, exactly in the middle of the sky -

interesting detail. Northbound from Maribor there will be a zone of total solar eclipse.

## WHAT IS IMPORTANT FOR THE THIRD WAVE?

For the third wave it is important that people know that this will be evacuation, they will trust the ships, which will be coming and they will not be afraid of the ships. It is important that they will release all attachments towards life on the Earth, towards material things, towards other people, that they would go upon ships, when the time is coming. And that they would not run heedlessly home to grab gold, jewelry, money, or children. Every individual that will be saved is important. That's why it is so important that people know what they will need to do at that time. So they would not fight the ships, shoot at them or run away from them. It is important that armies would not make any panic at that time, if there would be any armies remaining.

## HOW LONG WOULD THE EVACUATION LAST?

It will all occur very quickly, about 15 minutes for all humanity. So there will be no time for you to go home for jewelery, money, other people, souvenirs from holidays, but you would need to go on the ships immediately. Who'll run home and later come back, he will not find the ships anymore. And what is worse - because there will be earthquakes, floods, this will exterminate him. At the first sight, evacuation is strange, tragic, but actually it is not. After this transformation, Earth will be completely cleared, there will be no more pollution, and Earth will become an Eden like planet. People will also be cleared from all diseases, fears and pollution.

## HOW WILL PEOPLE LIVE AFTER THAT? IN A PHYSICAL BODY?

It depends on individual. Some of them will go to other planets that are already ready for those who would like to live in the world of duality or in physical body. Ships will transport

them to those planets. Some people will live as Ascended Masters on Earth, among them so called STAR PEOPLE. Some will go further on, on higher levels of existence.

**WHERE DID YOU GET THOSE VISIONS, THESE DATA?**

Some visions I received by my own, from within, some data I received from literature, so from different sources.

**WHEN AND WHY DID YOU BEGIN TO INTEREST IN THOSE THINGS?**

Very early I began to show interest for this, for cosmos. Since childhood I have a wish to go up, home. And this wish is slowly coming true.

**DO YOU REMEMBER YOUR HOME, YOUR PREVIOUS LIFES?**

Long before I first came to this planet, millions years ago, I lived on a planet named Alta or Ajaho in Pleiades. This was an etheric planet, where we lived as angelic beings. It was a very conscious life, about 15 to 18 million years ago. This information is correct because I received information from various sources and I harmonized it. Life on Alta, I remember very well, I could describe it as perfect happiness. In fact, we lived as one being, as angels. Angels know only happiness and joy.

**ARE THERE ANY MILESTONES IN YOUR CHILDHOOD, WHEN YOU BEGAN TO SHOW INTEREST FOR COSMOS?**

From the fifth year on I began to get interested in aircraft, and from 6th and 7th year I was very interested in space and space ships. I read science fiction a lot; I had astronomy as a hobby and later astrology. And now I'm making contact with Star beings.

## DO YOU HAVE CONTACT ALREADY?

I have or shall I rather say I am in a phase of establishing contact with them. I do not have firm contact yet. I am speaking of Star beings who don't live on this planet.

## DO YOU HAVE CONTACT WITH STAR BEINGS WHO LIVE UPON THIS PLANET?

Yes, I have contact with them. I know about 50 of them.

## HOW MANY STAR PEOPLE ARE IN SLOVENIA AND HOW MANY ON THE WHOLE EARTH?

I estimate about few thousands STAR PEOPLE in Slovenia, around the world there are about couple of hundred thousands to couple of millions. I do not know exactly.

## HOW DO YOU COMMUNICATE WITH THEM?

STAR PEOPLE are, looking from outside, just ordinary people, but they are working on self improvement, they are very interested in spirituality. Those who are in Slovenia I communicate with in Slovenian language, but lately we communicate also in Star language, with those who are enough aware.

## WHAT DOES STAR LANGUAGE LOOK LIKE?

It is a kind of angelic language. We are also developing telepathy, this ability is awakening spontaneously along with spiritual development, many abilities are developing which we'll need very much in the future.

## DO YOU HAVE CONTACTS WITH STAR PEOPLE WHO LIVE ANYWHERE ELSE IN THE WORLD?

I have contacts with Germany, Denmark, Netherlands and America.

## HOW DID YOU MAKE CONTACT WITH THEM?

I met some of them in Ireland, I wrote some letters to America to groups who are working with this and they wrote me back. We are now maintaining these connections.

## WHAT DO YOU REMEMBER FROM YOUR PREVIOUS LIFETIMES?

I remember many things - Atlantis, Egypt, India, Rome. This is my second time in Slovenia. I had 12 lifetimes. This is my last lifetime in physical body.

## WHAT IS YOUR MOST IMPORTANT MISSION IN THIS PERIOD TO CONTRIBUTE TO THE REALIZATION OF THE EVACUATION PLAN?

Currently I am spreading the information on Ascension waves and evacuation. The first and the second wave are called the Ascension waves. In the first and in the second wave the STAR PEOPLE will be evacuated, those who already were Masters and have a memory of that. Also Earth people can be evacuated those of them who are aware enough and know what is going on. And whoever will by freewill return to Earth will help by developing humanity and by the evacuation.

## WHAT ABOUT CIVILIZATIONS WHICH LIVE AMONG US BUT WE DON'T SEE THEM?

On the etheric plane there are many civilizations. Representatives of the Ashtar Command, Ascended Masters, who help the Earth, live freely among us - there is about 10 millions of them. All of them are members of GALACTIC CONFEDERATION, confederation of all planets of Light, all civilizations of Light, which help this planet and other planets also. Many of them came to Earth lately and there are also many ships around Earth which are ready for evacuation. Smaller ships are about few miles in diameter, but larger of them are also many of hundreds miles in diameter - these are mother-ships. The small ships are somewhat 10 meters in diameter, so called UFO. Those are materializing from etheric plane, when UFO appears suddenly but they are also in danger because Earth people have already shot at them. On the other way the physical plane is very dense and on this plane it is more difficult to carry out the maneuvers of flight. There are certain limitations on physical plane therefore it is much easier to travel, fly on the etheric plane. For instance, it is possible to travel through the centre of Earth. On the etheric plane there are also many neutral and positive beings, who are coming to this planet. Mostly they are scientific civilizations that are interested in life on this planet. Those beings are not harmful. For instance there are some beings coming from the part of Pleiades. When the Atlantis sank, a part of Atlantean civilization came back to Pleiades and they have established civilization which is more developed than the Earth one, but they have not yet ascended. They are interested in life on planet Earth. But there are also some negative beings; some of them are animal like. These are primitive beings. Those civilizations are abducting people but there are also some more negative civilizations which are also more dangerous. These are Dark Lords from Orion. They are involved on Earth from the time of Atlantis on, especially in the area of economy with credit cards, they are preparing total control through New world order etc.. Those Dark Lords are visible, they have a physical body.

## HOW THE POSITIVE CIVILIZATIONS ARE HELPING US?

They are sending us energy. A very important thing which is not yet visible from outside is that they are building the network of Light, on the etheric plane. That means that all atmosphere of the Earth or vibration of the humanity is rising. We are getting more optimistic. This has not yet manifested but there are some certain effects, for example peace movement, so called New Age, the end of the cold war between the former USSR and US.

## IS THERE A SURE DANGER OF OUTBURST OF THE ATOMIC WAR?

There is no danger for this anymore. There is a more definite danger of local wars around the Planet. Currently there is a crisis in Bosnia, wherefrom the war can spread all over Europe. There is also definite danger in the former USSR.

## WHAT IS THE FINAL GOAL OF ALL COSMOS, OF ALL CIVILIZATIONS?

The final goal is an evolution which will lead towards perfection, happiness and oneness. At the end there will be a reunification as there once was a separation. So now we have known separation and we can go back consciously. This is a purpose of all.

## WHAT ARE YOUR PLANS IN THE NEAR FUTURE?

I am going to Los Angeles and I do not know if I am coming back to Slovenia.

## WHY ARE YOU GOING TO AMERICA? YOU HAVE A GROUP THERE?

I don't have a group, these are only my visions. Actually I am searching for a certain group in Los Angeles. I am connected with that group since the time of Atlantis; we all came from the planet Alta, where we lived as one being. Later we separated but not totally, because we were connected through all the lifetimes. There is a girl, who is my twin soul and is also connected with this group. I saw her in a vision 10 years ago, she is calling me and that's why I am leaving.

## DOES ANYBODY HAVE ITS TWIN SOUL?

Before we came first to planet Earth we were together with our twin souls. Later we separated and each of us lived its own life. Each had its own experiences.

## THE TOTALITY IS MAN AND WOMAN TOGETHER?

Actually this is one soul which incarnates in two bodies. Male and female. The occult law says that before they become Masters, in their last lifetimes they come together. So now I will meet her. Having contact with a twin soul is something very beautiful. It is an energy we search all our lifetimes. If you don't have this connection there is always something missing. And once you have this connection, life becomes much easier.

## HOW CAN YOU MAKE CONNECTION WITH YOUR TWIN SOUL?

With meditation. You visualize his or her image. You visualize your ideal because all ideals emerge from the memory of life with twin soul. Both poles call each other. And this creates very strong energetic vortex and there comes a moment when you can not deny this call, you need to go, regardless of everything.

## HOW WILL YOU RECOGNIZE THIS GIRL?

I know how her physical body looks like; I know how her voice looks like though I haven't met her yet. I know her very well and I would recognize her immediately.

## WHAT IS IF ONE POLE IS ON EARTH, OTHER ONE ON THE OTHER PLANET?

In this case the soul mate will channel the energy of twin soul and this is something very similar. Everybody on a spiritual path will meet his twin soul or at least a soul mate. It is because on this planet, on Earth, energy of Oneness needs to be established. And this is very important. This is why we came on Earth from other planets, because we can bring this energy here. We know it already, we have been in Oneness and even though we've lost the memory of it we can still remember much sooner. We can achieve Oneness much easier. We brought this energy to Earth and therefore humanity can develop much faster as would otherwise.

## WHAT ARE THE RELATIONS BETWEEN THE SPACE BEINGS?

All are cooperating very harmonically; each has his own position regarding his own talents and inclinations. This is not a hard work and each of them is doing his work with joy. There are many of them around Earth right now. Ashtar Command is a fleet of space ships around this planet and Ashtar SherAn is its commander.

## CAN YOU SEE THEM?

I do not see them, but I receive visions. I have seen many times the ships landing on this planet at evacuation. I have not seen them directly, at least until now. A vision is in one way an impression, a picture, this is not etheric seeing, but it is similar. So in one way I can say I see them.

## CAN MANY PEOPLE SEE THEM?

Some can see them. It is very interesting because things agree together. What I have seen, other have seen also. So things are confirming this way and this is very important.

## WHY ATLANTIS SANK?

Atlantis sank four times. The first and the second time this was a natural disaster, but the third and the fourth time it went down because of the crystal experiments. The purpose of these cataclysms was the same as it is now - purification of Earth.

Civilization went away from its right path. Something less than million years ago Dark Lords from Orion came to Earth. Orion is a constellation, and those Dark Lords are from the star which is called Rigel. They came to Earth to bring confusion. There were intense wars on Atlantis and because of the wars between the Black and the White Magicians Atlantis went down. This was famous fall from Eden.

Looking from a higher perspective, the sinking of Atlantis was incorporated in Divine Plan, also the Black Magicians came to Earth with permission from Ashtar. So duality could play out and then clear completely, otherwise it couldn't. There were intense wars and genetic misuses on Atlantis; like now, even though it was much more widespread in those times. In its late period - last 200 thousands years' earth time, Atlantis was very highly developed, because much knowledge came from Pleiades.

Space ships were landing as planes do now, but they didn't use atomic energy because it is a very unclear source of energy. They knew materialization, space travel, telepathy. After deluge nothing of that remained.

## IS THE BERMUDA TRIANGLE ALSO CONNECTED WITH ATLANTIS?

Below the sea, a crystal generator remained which distorts the magnetic field. Some sort of null zone was created, which causes the changes of space time continuum structure. A vortex was created which can send you on etheric plane, in past, in future, other space and time. This is area around the Bermuda triangle.

## HOW THE NEGATIVE CIVILIZATIONS LIKE THE BLACK MAGICIANS WERE DEVELOPED?

Beings from Orion are in fact fallen angels, they have been ascended before. They went through similar process as we do but they have lost their consciousness much more. Part of their origin is still a mystery which must not be revealed. They went to the core of the matter; they went consciously in total separation. If we look back into evolution - when this Universe was manifested, a part of God decided to be separated from itself. And beings from Orion are originating from that part. They are needed, they are part of the Divine Plan, they are doing their mission. Many of them will be saved at the evacuation, many of them will not. Those of them who'd like to continue to spread all negativity will die as a soul also.

## WHAT IS THE PURPOSE OF RELIGION?

Which regards religion very important is trust. People would not look so much to the external form of religion - who died on a cross and why - but have to trust in something higher. The changes which will manifest in those years on Earth will cause much chaos, because people do not have knowledge of what will happen. In the midst of this chaos people need to keep trust in the higher wisdom, in the higher guidance.

## ARE THE LEADERSHIPS OF VARIOUS RELIGIONS - LIKE CHRISTIANITY OR ISLAM - AWARE OF THE PLAN, ARE THEY ACCEPTING IT?

If they are aware, certainly they do not dare to do anything about it.

## IS THIS PLAN REPRESENTED IN THE APOCALYPSE ALREADY?

If people would follow that which is written in the Scriptures, where everything is shown very clearly, everything would be much more simple. It is enough for us to know the New Testament, where there are every signs of the evacuation.

## WHAT RELIGION WILL EMERGE IN FEW YEARS?

It will not be a religion in the present sense of this word; it will be some kind of esoteric psychology. This will be a knowing about God, religion, which bases on realization. And this is esoteric. Realization that Man, in his essence, is God.

## WHAT IS GOD? WHAT IS FREEWILL?

This can actually not be said. God is love. People are imagining God as a person. But which is more important is enlightenment, direct experience. Everything before enlightenment is just guessing, ideas, and conceptions. Man needs to experience enlightenment. Until that, faith and trust are very important. Trust in a Plan and in that current happening on Earth has a higher sense, that there will be the evacuation, that this chaos does not mean the end of the world, but just a great transformation.

Cataclysms are actually just cleansing in line with the law of the nature. Nobody needs to die on this planet, but many will rather decide to die, instead of leaving anything on Earth. Everybody could be saved with his freewill; the ships are ready for everybody on this planet. Even for murderers, for everybody with freewill.

## HOW LONG WOULD WE LIVE UPON THE SHIPS? AND LIFE AFTER?

It depends on how long the Earth will be cleansing itself. Earth will be cleansing itself few years, even though the transformation will be very short. The cataclysm itself will take maybe a few days. And I think it will take only few seconds. It will be a moment which can not be described, which can not be measured by time. The whole structure of matter will change dramatically - there will be a leap in higher dimension, in just one moment. We will not measure time in earth years anymore. And if we would measure in current earth time, I estimate, the cleansing would take about 13 years, and some people estimate 5 to 7 years. Right after the cataclysm Ascended Masters will come to Earth and begin to cleanse the planet. People mostly will not come back, but will come to other planets, where they could live as they have lived on Earth. Life will be much easier for them, because there will be no Dark Lords any more. There will be no more famine or wars, in a current sense of the word, it will be much easier as it is now.

## WHAT KIND OF LITERATURE ABOUT EVACUATION IS ACCESSIBLE IN SLOVENIA?

There are various books, articles, there is not much literature. In America, a book was published, which speaks about the first and the second wave. Information is coming through various sources and channels.

## WHAT IS THE ROLE OF SLOVENIA IN THIS PLAN?

Slovenia is a very important point, because it is just right near the dangerous area in Bosnia. There is a rift in aura, a weak point, from where conflicts could spread all over Europe. Slovenia is a buffer against those conflicts and they will not spread from thereon. Slovenia is protected from up high, it is protected very strongly energetically, and there will be peace until the major transformation. In Slovenia the information about the evacuation will begin to spread around. The surface of Slovenia is small, the population is small also and so the critical mass will be achieved quickly.

## IS SLOVENIA IMPORTANT FOR THE QUANTUM LEAP OF CONSCIOUSNESS?

This quantum leap of consciousness in Slovenia has happened already. Information about the evacuation has spread all around the land. This means that Slovenia is saved already, actually Slovene people are saved. So people will be ready for evacuation when time comes. Because the quantum leap has occurred already - on the 14th of September 1993. Slovenia is a vortex of New Age, there are 12 of them all around the world, and these are currently the most important points on Earth, which regards consciousness.

## WHAT INFLUENCED THE QUANTUM LEAP OF CONSCIOUSNESS IN SLOVENIA?

Information about the evacuation spread all around. We have spread that information for the last half of year and critical mass was achieved quickly. In Slovenia there are about 500 people who are engaged in the New Age movement; from those people around 30 to 40 people need to know about the evacuation and the Ascension waves. And those 500 people knew this somewhat and when they read an article about the evacuation they were ready for it. Something shifted in their consciousness and if 500 people know soon 3000 people know. And when 3000 people know Slovenia is saved. They know somehow, consciously or subconsciously. When the time comes they will be ready. That's why those messages need to spread around now. And when the whole Slovenia will know, soon the whole world will know. It is spreading like fire. It started in Slovenia and it can not be stopped. Slovenia is, in fact, some kind of a trigger.

# Appendix

# NEW ATLANTIS

The purpose of the project is to anchor on the physical plane the ideal of coming civilization, which will blend the best from the old Atlantis (view into the past) with all hopes and aspirations of the One which leads humanity into a better world (view into the future). New Atlantis will be a civilization which humanity will create during the transition into the New age - the age of Aquarius.

In the initial phase the project consists of three subprojects:

1) TIME-SPACE LITHOPUNCTURE

Lithopuncture is healing of the energy body of planet Earth with stone statues and sculptures. Time-space lithopuncture heals time-space anomaly that planet Earth is subjected to, with the aid of meditative awakening of universal remembrance. In Graeco-Roman sculptures and some other objects from that time period there is an energetic imprint of ideal of old Atlantis in their subatomic structure. If we put such statue or object on a specific spot and enliven the energetic memory which dwells within it with meditation, such object or statue becomes alive and its energy field begins to emanate a message about the ideal of old Atlantis into surrounding space.

2) ACTIVATION, ENLIVENING AND HEALING OF PLANETARY VORTICES

Before the civilization of New Atlantis can manifest on the physical plane it must become alive in energetic world, in world of archetypes. Planetary vortices are angelic beings who are on special energy spots throughout the world preparing the living organism of Earth for the great change that is awaiting this planet. With specific meditation work we can enliven these angelic vortices and with suitable anchors (aquamarine crystals) we connect them with the physical plane so that they begin to accelerate the evolution of humanity and prepare the consciousness of people for arrival of New Atlantis. With certain specific crystal opals we connect those planetary vortices with the tachyon energy field that is coming to this planet from interstellar space and thus enliven and heal them.

The following activations of dimensional portals are planned:

Thule, Greenland
Palmdale/Lancaster, CA
Mojave, CA
Mount Shasta, CA
Azores
Antigua, Little Antiles
Aramu Muru, Peru
Altiplano, Bolivia
Easter Island
McMurdo, Antarctica
Vostok Lake, Antarctica
Maupiti, Bora Bora, Tetiaroa, Rangiroa, Society Islands
Cook Islands
Whitsundays, Australia
Uluru, Australia
Coober Pedy, Australia
Lightning Ridge, Australia
Avebury, Great Britain

Scedro, Croatia
Most na Soci, Slovenia
Tivoli, Ljubljana, Slovenia
Paestum, Italy
Verona, Venice, Italy
Santorini, Knossos, Stymfalia, Greece
Ahaggar, Algeria
Gizeh, Luxor, Egypt
Mt. Kailash, Tibet
Soda Plains, Tibet
Fujijama, Japan
The Pamirs
Skardu, Gilgit, Pakistan

3) PUBLISHING OF THE ENGLISH VERSION OF ASCENSION BOOK now titled "Aurora 2012" A Manual For Preparedness (author Ishtar Antares)

This book contains basic information needed for awakening of humanity and its preparation for entry into the New Age.

In the next phase the project anticipates building a network of temples on specific points around the planet, where awakening (transmission of correct esoteric information), anchoring of energies (dimensional lithopuncture), healing (deactivation of old Atlantean implants) and merger (galactic tantra) will be taking place. Knowledge that is needed for this is already available, all that is needed is physical realization of the project. The Atlantean network is supporting the project with its energy. The project will be carried out according to available financial resources acquired from sponsors.

Speed of project's manifestation will reflect the state of consciousness on planet Earth. When the network of light, created with the project, will be strong enough, it will enable contact with forces of light such as Atlantean network and Resistance movement and through time also with positive extraterrestrial civilizations.

Sponsors interested in the project can reach the author at antarion@volja.net

Note: The following are outlines as to the live seminars presented worldwide by Ishtar Antares. Those interested in organizing a workshop in their local area can contact the author at antarion@volja.net

# AURORA WORKSHOP

## By ISHTAR ANTARES

We are living in extraordinary times. This world is about to enter a totally new dimension, a new reality, an end of linear time. Are you ready? This workshop is a detailed introduction to preparedness...

Friday 7 p.m. to 9 p.m......................INTRODUCTION

Saturday 10 a.m. to 2 p.m. ................... PLANETARY LIGHTWORK

- -History of the Universe, Galactic wars and Atlantis
- -Planetary and extraplanetary forces of Light
- -New World Order - and how it will fall apart
- -AURORA: divine plan for the New Age
- -Galactic Wave of love and tachyon energy
- -Planetary light grid healing

Saturday 4 p.m. to 8 p.m. ..................... ASCENSION TRAINING

- -Your mission – life you were born to live
- -Initiations and path of evolution
- -Emotional vibrational healing, kundalini and Samadhi experiences
- -Deprogramming of consciousness

Sunday 10 a.m. to 2 p.m. ...................... LIGHT BODY ACTIVATION

- -Light body activation
- -One heart, One eye and Galactic core
- -Ascension Column
- -Living in abundance: law of manifestation

Sunday 4 p.m. to 8 p.m. ....................... MANDALA OF SOULS

- -Group Ascension process
- -Twin souls, Soulmates and Soul families
- -Relationships of duality and relationships of Oneness
- -Islands of Light

# GALACTIC TANTRA

## By ISHTAR ANTARES

The magnetic attraction between female and male polarity that sparks the rise of kundalini energy is the ultimate mystery of the universe. The sensual loving energy from which worlds were born. Let's take the journey to the center of the mystery...

FRIDAY , 7 p.m. to 9 p.m. ................INTRODUCTION

SATURDAY, 10 a.m. to 6 p.m. ......MODULE I : GALACTIC TANTRA

*Soul origins: stargates and planet Earth experience
*Healing the split between Soul and personality (fear, risk, safety and freedom)
*God/Goddess archetypes
*Healing the split between love and sexuality (removing sexuality implants:pleasure and the Soul)
*One living mandala
*Twin souls, soul mates and soul families
*Planetary tantric lightwork

SUNDAY, 10 a.m. to 6 p.m. ......MODULE II: RETURN OF THE GODDESS

*Soul infused relationships
*Mysteries of the Goddess
*Priesthood of sacred sexuality
*Deprogramming from patriarchal society
*Kundalini awakening (cosmic orgasm and Samadhi experiences)
*Healing with loving erotic energy
*Tibetan healing tantric massage

# THE SECRET OF ABUNDANCE

By ISHTAR ANTARES

The dream house near the ocean. Traveling around the world in a private jet. Sharing precious moments of love with your perfect mate. Following your bliss not working for money but manifesting your divine purpose and assisting the planet while getting rich during the process. Expanding your horizons beyond your wildest dreams. All this can be yours and is intended to be yours in the life you were meant to live...

Friday 7 p.m. to 9 p.m...............................INTRODUCTION

Saturday 10 a.m. to 2 p.m. .... LAW OF MANIFESTATION

-Abundance consciousness
-Esotheric principles of manifestation
-Decision-invocation-action
-Next step spiritual technology

Saturday 4 p.m. to 6 p.m. DISCOVERING YOUR PURPOSE

-Your mission - life you were born to live
-Expressing your flow
-Your wish is a divine command

Sunday 10 a.m. to 2 p.m. ..................... LIFE TREASURE MAP

-Demanifestation filters
-Vortex support field
-Reality shaping

Sunday 4 p.m. to 6 p.m. ................................... MONEY FLOW

-Creating money flow
-Removing blocks of poverty
-Internet and abundance

## TACHYON JEWELRY FOR SPIRITUAL GROWTH AND ASCENSION

Tachyons are subatomic particles that travel faster than light. They are particles that infuse physical matter with spiritual light. Tachionization is a technological process that impregnates the physical matter with an increased quantity of tachyons in a special chamber and thus it permanently changes quantum properties of atomic nuclei which compose that matter. Tachyon jewelry is a very powerful spiritual growth, light body activation and ascension accelerator and is one of the most powerful tools ever created for our ascension process. Precious opal, diamond and tanzanite, set in silver, gold, platinum or palladium provides the optimal combination of energies for very high spiritual frequency acceleration.

**Contact Ishtar about his Tachyon jewelry at**

**antarion@volja.net**

**(Or www.jewelinthelotus.info)**

Michele Blood says *"The beautiful jewelry that has been Tachionized is simply amazing grace. The energy I felt when I first wore my pendant was a Divine Current going straight through my heart and crown charkras. I also have the Tachionization cubes next to my computer. I do indeed highly recommend this for anyone wishing to have a harmonious frequency."*